I, STEVE

I, STEVE

Steve Jobs In His Own Words

EDITED BY GEORGE BEAHM

AN AGATE IMPRINT

CHICAGO

I, Steve is in no way authorized, prepared, approved, or endorsed by
Steve Jobs and is not affiliated with or endorsed by any of his past or
present organizations.

First edition November 2011

ISBN-10 1-932841-66-0

ISBN-13 978-1-932841-66-4

Printed in the United States.

10   9   8   7   6   5   4   3   2   1

B2 Books is an imprint of Agate Publishing, Inc. Agate books are available in bulk at discount prices. For more information, go to agatepub-
lishing.com.

TABLE OF CONTENTS

This one is for Britton Edwards.

Apple has a core set of talents, and those talents are: We do, I think, very good hardware design; we do very good industrial design; and we write very good system and application software. And we're really good at packaging that all together into a product. We're the only people left in the computer industry that do that.

—STEVE JOBS,
INTERVIEWED BY JEFF GOODELL, "STEVE
JOBS: THE ROLLING STONE INTERVIEW,"
ROLLING STONE #684, JUNE 16, 1994

INTRODUCTION
Steve Jobs and the "Vision Thing"

I'm always keeping my eyes open for the next big opportunity, but the way the world is now, it will take enormous resources, both in money and in engineering talent, to make it happen. I don't know what that next big thing might be, but I have a few ideas.

—STEVE JOBS
ON THE "NEXT BIG THING", *CNNMONEY*,
JANUARY 24, 2000

Since 1976 Steve Jobs has always spoken his mind, to the delight of his advocates and the dismay of his detractors, in every possible venue: press releases, statements on Apple's Websites, public appearances to introduce new Apple products, and interviews to the print and electronic media.

But no matter what one thinks of Jobs, who twice cites "the vision thing" on his résumé, one indisputable fact stands out: He has given us some of the most memorable quotes about the nature of business in our time.

Steve Jobs occupies a unique and enviable position in the business community. He has been selected as "CEO of the Decade" by *Fortune* magazine, the "world's best-performing CEO" by the *Harvard Business Review*, and "Person of the Decade" by the *Wall Street Journal*, among numerous other honors.

On August 18, 2011, news broke that the only authorized biography of Steve Jobs, written by Walter Isaacson, curiously had been moved up from March 2012 to November 21, 2011, prompting questions as to why. Big publishers simply don't move up pub dates four months on a whim. Clearly, a shoe had been dropped.

Six days later, on August 24, the other shoe dropped: Steve Jobs announced he was stepping down as CEO, and asked the Apple board to "execute our succession plan," which put Timothy Cook at the helm.

As with his longtime business rival and friend, Bill Gates, Steve Jobs decided to leave at the top of his game, likely influenced by health issues. Both business computer pioneers have, as the world has, moved on; the companies they started changed the world, and they both recognized that it was time for others to take the reins.

There is only one Steve Jobs, and it is his unique vision that fundamentally changed five highly competitive, interrelated industries. It seems fitting, then, that as he stepped down from the company he founded and passionately loves, we look back to see Apple through his unique perspective, and in his own words culled from public announcements and media interviews over the last thirty-five years.

QUOTATIONS

••

Anxiety before iPad Debut

Even though we've been using these internally
for some time and working on it for a few years,
you still have butterflies in your stomach the
week before…the night before introduction…the
launch…. You never know until you get it into
your customers' hands and they tell you what they
think. The feedback we've got has been off the
charts. We think this is a profound game-changer.
We think when people look back some number of
years from now, they'll see this as a major event
in personal computation devices. What's been
really great for me is how quickly people have got
it. You know, I've gotten a few thousand emails
from people I've never talked to before just telling
me how much they think this product is going to
change their life and what they do. People are getting it very quickly.

—*Apple event for iPhone 4.0 software, April 8, 2010*

....

Apple's Core: Employees

All we are is our ideas, or people. That's what keeps us going to work in the morning, to hang around these great bright people. I've always thought that recruiting is the heart and soul of what we do.

—D5 Conference: All Things Digital, May 30, 2007

....

Apple's DNA

Most of us can't wait to get to work in the morning. But it's not like Apple has somehow morphed into a mass-market consumer electronics company. Our DNA hasn't changed. It's that mass-market consumer electronics is turning into Apple.

—CNNMoney/Fortune, February 21, 2005

Apple's Existence

What if Apple didn't exist? Think about it. *Time* wouldn't get published next week. Some 70% of the newspapers in the U.S. wouldn't publish tomorrow morning. Some 60% of the kids wouldn't have computers; 64% of the teachers wouldn't have computers. More than half the Websites created on Macs wouldn't exist. So there's something worth saving here. See?

—Time, *August 18, 1997*

Attention Getting

And one more thing...

—Characteristically used toward the end of Apple events

Being the Best

We're not going to be the first to this party, but we're going to be the best.

—Apple event for iPhone OS 4.0, April 8, 2010

● ●

Beyond Recruiting

It's not just recruiting. After recruiting, it's building an environment that makes people feel they are surrounded by equally talented people and their work is bigger than they are. The feeling that the work will have tremendous influence and is part of a strong, clear vision—all those things. Recruiting usually requires more than you alone can do, so I've found that collaborative recruiting and having a culture that recruits the "A" players is the best way. Any interviewee will speak with at least a dozen people in several areas of this company, not just those in the area that he would work in. That way a lot of your "A" employees get broad exposure to the company, and—by having a company culture that supports them if they feel strongly enough—the current employees can veto a candidate.

—In the Company of Giants, *1997*

....

Branding

We don't stand a chance of advertising with features and benefits and with RAMs and with charts and comparisons. The only chance we have of communicating is with a feeling.

—The Apple Way, 2006

What are the great brands? Levi's, Coke, Disney, Nike. Most people would put Apple in that category. You could spend billions of dollars building a brand not as good as Apple. Yet Apple hasn't been doing anything with this incredible asset. What is Apple, after all? Apple is about people who think "outside the box," people who want to use computers to help them change the world, to help them create things that make a difference, and not just to get a job done.

—Time, *August 18, 1997*

∙∙

Broad-Based Education

Reed College at that time offered perhaps the best calligraphy instruction in the country.... I decided to take a calligraphy class to learn how to do this.... It was beautiful, historical, artistically subtle in a way that science can't capture, and I found it fascinating. None of this had even a hope of any practical application in my life. But ten years later, when we were designing the first Macintosh computer, it all came back to me.

—Commencement address, Stanford University,
June 12, 2005

∙∙

Broad Life Experiences, Importance of

A lot of people in our industry haven't had very diverse experiences. So they don't have enough dots to connect, and they end up with very linear solutions without a broad perspective on the problem. The broader one's understanding of the human experience, the better design we will have.

—Wired, *February 1996*

∙∙

Company Focus

We do no market research. We don't hire consultants…. We just want to make great products.

—*CNNMoney*/Fortune, *February 2008*

∙∙

Competition

After Apple management complained about the six Apple employees SJ was taking with him to start NeXT: I wasn't aware that Apple owned me, you know. I don't think they do. I think that I own me. And for me not to be able to practice my craft ever again in my life seems odd. We're not going to take any technology, any proprietary ideas out of Apple. We're willing to put that in writing. It's the law, anyway. There is nothing, by the way, that says Apple can't compete with us if they think what we're doing is such a great idea. It's hard to think that a $2 billion company with 4,300+ people couldn't compete with six people in blue jeans.

—Newsweek, *September 30, 1985*

···

Computers

The problem is, in hardware you can't build a computer that's twice as good as anyone else's anymore. Too many people know how to do it. You're lucky if you do one that's one-and-a-third times better or one-and-a-half times better. And then it's only six months before everybody else catches up.

—Rolling Stone, *June 16, 1994*

···

Computers for Everyman

The roots of Apple were to build computers for people, not for corporations. The world doesn't need another Dell or Compaq.

—Time, *October 18, 1999*

···

Computers as Tools

What a computer is to me is the most remarkable tool that we have ever come up with. It's the equivalent of a bicycle for our minds.

—Memory & Imagination, *1990*

••

Confusing Product Lines

What I found when I got here was a zillion and one products. It was amazing. And I started to ask people, now why would I recommend a 3400 over a 4400? When should somebody jump up to a 6500, but not a 7300? And after three weeks, I couldn't figure this out. If I couldn't figure this out...how could our customers figure this out?

—*Apple Worldwide Developers Conference, 1998*

••

Consumerism

I end up not buying a lot of things, because I find them ridiculous.

—The Independent, *October 29, 2005*

We spent some time in our family talking about what's the trade-off we want to make. We ended up talking a lot about design, but also about the values of our family. Did we care most about getting our wash done in an hour versus an hour and a half? Or did we care most about our clothes feeling really soft and lasting longer? Did we care about using a quarter of the water? We spent two weeks talking about this every night at the dinner table. We'd get around to that old washer-dryer discussion. And the talk was about design.

—Wired, *February 1996*

....

Consumer Product Design

Re: the iPod—Look at the design of a lot of con-sumer products—they're really complicated sur-faces. We tried to make something much more holistic and simple. When you first start off trying to solve a problem, the first solutions you come up with are very complex, and most people stop there. But if you keep going, and live with the problem and peel more layers of the onion off, you can oftentimes arrive at some very elegant and simple solutions. Most people just don't put in the time or energy to get there. We believe that cus-tomers are smart and want objects which are well thought through.

—Newsweek, *October 14, 2006*

....

Contribution

It was one of the first times I started thinking that maybe Thomas Edison did a lot more to improve the world than Karl Marx and [Hindu guru] Neem Karoli Baba put together.

—Steve Jobs: The Brilliant Mind Behind Apple, *2009*

· ·

Convergence

The place where Apple has been standing for the last two decades is exactly where computer technology and the consumer electronics markets are converging. So it's not like we're having to cross the river to go somewhere else; the other side of the river is coming to us.

—*CNNMoney*/Fortune, *February 21, 2005*

· ·

Creating New Tools

We make tools for people. Tools to create, tools to communicate. The age we're living in, these tools surprise you.... That's why I love what we do. Because we make these tools, and we're constantly surprised with what people do with them.

—*D5 Conference: All Things Digital, 2007*

• •

Creativity and Technology

One of the things I learned at Pixar is the technology industries and the content industries do not understand each other. In Silicon Valley and at most technology companies, I swear that most people think the creative process is a bunch of guys in their early 30s, sitting on a couch, drinking beer and thinking of jokes. No, they really do. That's how television is made, they think; that's how movies are made. People in Hollywood and in the content industries, they think technology is something you just write a check for and buy. They don't understand the creativity element of technology. These are like ships passing in the night.

—CNN Tech, June 10, 2011

....

Credo

It's Not Done Until It Ships.

—*Folklore.org, January 1983*

The Journey Is the Reward.

—*Folklore.org, January 1983*

The organization is clean and simple to understand, and very accountable. Everything just got simpler. That's been one of my mantras—focus and simplicity.

—Bloomberg Businessweek, *May 12, 1998*

Customer Complaints

I have received hundreds of emails from iPhone customers who are upset about Apple dropping the price of iPhone by $200 two months after it went on sale. After reading every one of these emails, I have some observations and conclusions.... There is always change and improvement, and there is always someone who bought a product before a particular cutoff date and misses the new price or the new operating system or the new whatever. This is life in the technology lane. If you always wait for the next price cut or to buy the new improved model, you'll never buy any technology product because there is always something better and less expensive on the horizon.... [E]ven though we are making the right decision to lower the price of iPhone, and even though the technology road is bumpy, we need to do a better job of taking care of our early iPhone customers as we aggressively go after new ones with a lower price. Our early customers trusted us, and we must live up to that trust with our actions in moments like these.

—*Apple Website, September 2007*

••

Customer Loyalty

I get asked a lot why Apple's customers are so loyal. It's not because they belong to the Church of Mac! That's ridiculous.

It's because when you buy our products, and three months later you get stuck on something, you quickly figure out [how to get past it]. And you think, "Wow, someone over there at Apple actually thought of this!".... There's almost no product in the world that you have that experience with, but you have it with a Mac. And you have it with an iPod.

—Bloomberg Businessweek, *October 12, 2004*

••

David versus Goliath

It's curious to me that the largest computer company in the world [IBM] couldn't even match the Apple II, which was designed in a garage six years ago.

—InfoWorld, *March 8, 1982*

••

Deadlines

No way, there's no way we're slipping! You guys
have been working on this stuff for months now.
Another couple of weeks isn't going to make that
much of a difference. You may as well get it over
with. Just make it as good as you can. You better
get back to work!

—Folklore.org, January 1984

Real artists ship.

—Folklore.org, January 1984

Death

That's why I think death is the most wonderful invention of life. It purges the system of these old models that are obsolete. I think that's one of Apple's challenges, really. When two young people walk in with the next thing, are we going to embrace it and say this is fantastic? Are you going to be willing to drop our models, or are we going to explain it away? I think we'll do better, because we're completely aware of it and we make it a priority.

—Playboy, *February 1985*

Quoting Mark Twain, on the premature announcement of his death by Bloomberg: The reports of my death are greatly exaggerated.

—*Apple event for the iPod, September 9, 2008*

· ·

Decision Making

At Apple, there are ten *really* important decisions
to make every week. It's a transactional company;
it's got a lot of new products every month. And
if some of those decisions are wrong, maybe you
can fix them a few months later. At Pixar, because
I'm not directing the movies, there are just a few
really important strategic decisions to make every
month, maybe even every quarter, but they're
really hard to change. Pixar's much slower-paced,
but you can't change your mind when you go
down these paths.

—To Infinity and Beyond! *2007*

· ·

Demise

Apple has some tremendous assets, but I believe
without some attention, the company could,
could, could—I'm searching for the right word—
could, could die.

—Time, *August 18, 1997*

· ·

Dent In the Universe

Being the richest man in the cemetery doesn't matter to me.... Going to bed at night saying we've done something wonderful—that's what matters to me.

—*CNNMoney*/Fortune, *May 25, 1993*

· ·

Design

In most people's vocabularies, design means veneer. It's interior decorating. It's the fabric of the curtains and the sofa. But to me, nothing could be further from the meaning of design. Design is the fundamental soul of a man-made creation that ends up expressing itself in successive outer layers of the product or service.

—*CNNMoney*/Fortune, *January 24, 2000*

Design is a funny word. Some people think design means how it looks. But of course, if you dig deeper, it's really how it works. The design of the Mac wasn't what it looked like, although that was part of it. Primarily, it was how it worked. To design something really well, you have to get it. You have to really grok what it's all about. It takes a passionate commitment to really thoroughly understand something, chew it up, not just quickly swallow it. Most people don't take the time to do that.

—Wired, *February 1996*

Look at the Mercedes design, the proportion of sharp detail to flowing lines. Over the years they've made the design softer but the details starker. That's what we have to do with the Macintosh.

—Odyssey: Pepsi to Apple, *1987*

Difference, the Essential

The Lisa people wanted to do something great. And the Mac people want to do something insanely great. The difference shows.

—*Apple Confidential 2.0, 2004*

Disney's Animated Movie Sequels

We feel sick about Disney doing sequels, because if you look at the quality of their sequels, like *The Lion King 1.5* and [*Return to Never Land*], it's pretty embarrassing.

—*Associated Press, 2004*

E-Book Readers

I'm sure there will always be dedicated devices, and they may have a few advantages in doing just one thing. But I think the general-purpose devices will win the day. Because I think people just probably aren't willing to pay for a dedicated device.

—New York Times, *September 9, 2009*

• •

Employee Motivation

We attract a different type of person—a person who doesn't want to wait five or ten years to have someone take a giant risk on him or her. Someone who really wants to get in a little over his head and make a little dent in the universe.

—Playboy, *February 1985*

• •

Employee Potential

My job is not to be easy on people. My job is to make them better.

—*CNNMoney.com*/Fortune, *February 2008*

• •

Excellence

People judge you by your performance, so focus on the outcome. Be a yardstick of quality. Some people aren't used to an environment where excellence is expected.

—Steve Jobs: The Journey is the Reward, *1987*

....

Excitement

We designed iMac to deliver the things consumers care about most—the excitement of the Internet and the simplicity of the Mac. iMac is next year's computer for $1,299, not last year's computer for $999.

—Apple Confidential 2.0, *2004*

....

Firing Employees

It's painful when you have some people who are not the best people in the world and you have to get rid of them; but I found my job has sometimes exactly been that—to get rid of some people who didn't measure up and I've always tried to do it in a humane way. But nonetheless it has to be done and it is never fun.

—*Smithsonian Institution Oral and Video Histories,*
April 20, 1995

....

Flash Crash

Symantec recently highlighted Flash for having one of the worst security records in 2009. We also know firsthand that Flash is the number-one reason Macs crash. We have been working with Adobe to fix these problems, but they have persisted for several years now. We don't want to reduce the reliability and security of our iPhones, iPods and iPads by adding Flash.... Flash was created during the PC era—for PCs and mice. Flash is a successful business for Adobe, and we can understand why they want to push it beyond PCs. But the mobile era is about low-power devices, touch interfaces, and open web standards—all areas where Flash falls short.

—*Apple Website, April 2010*

· ·

Focus

People think focus means saying *yes* to the thing you've got to focus on. But that's not what it means at all. It means saying *no* to the hundred other good ideas that there are. You have to pick carefully. I'm actually as proud of the things we haven't done as the things I have done. Innovation is saying *no* to 1,000 things.

—Apple Worldwide Developers Conference,
May 13–16, 1997

· ·

Focusing on Product

In response to the question, "What can we learn from Apple's struggle to innovate during the de-cade before you returned in 1997?" You need a very product-oriented culture, even in a technology company. Lots of companies have tons of great engineers and smart people. But ultimately, there needs to be some gravitational force that pulls it all together. Otherwise, you can get great pieces of technology all floating around the universe. But it doesn't add up to much.

—Bloomberg Businessweek, *October 12, 2004*

Sure, what we do has to make commercial sense, but it's never the starting point. We start with the product and the user experience.

—Time, *April 1, 2010*

···

Forcing the Issue

What happened was, the designers came up with this really great idea. Then they take it to the engineers, and the engineers go, "Nah, we can't do that. That's impossible." And so it gets a lot worse. Then they take it to the manufacturing people, and they go, "We can't build that!" And it gets a lot worse.... Sure enough, when we took it to the engineers, they said, "Oh." And they came up with 38 reasons. And I said, "No, no, we're doing this." And they said, "Well, why?" And I said, "Because I'm the CEO and I think it can be done." And so they kind of begrudgingly did it. But then it was a big hit."

—Time, *October 16, 2005*

∙∙∙

Forward Thinking

If you want to live your life in a creative way, as an artist, you have to not look back too much. You have to be willing to take whatever you've done and whoever you were and throw them away.

—Playboy, *February 1985*

Let's go invent tomorrow rather than worrying about what happened yesterday.

—D5 *Conference: All Things Digital, May 30, 2007*

∙∙∙

Getting It Right

On redesigning the Apple store layout by "solution zones," after employees initially protested, "Do you know what you're saying? Do you know we have to start over?" It cost us, I don't know, six, nine months. But it was the right decision by a million miles.

—*CNNMoney/*Fortune, *March 8, 2007*

●●

Goals

When we first started Apple we really built the first computer because we wanted one. We designed this crazy new computer with color and a whole bunch of other things called the Apple II which you have probably heard about. We had a passion to do this one simple thing which was to get a bunch of computers to our friends so they could have as much fun with them as we were.

—Return to the Little Kingdom, *2009*

●●

Grace Under Pressure

Many times in an interview I will purposely upset someone: I'll criticize their prior work. I'll do my homework, find out what they worked on, and say, "God, that really turned out to be a bomb. That really turned out to be a bozo product. Why did you work on that?..." I want to see what people are like under pressure. I want to see if they just fold or if they have firm conviction, belief, and pride in what they did.

—In the Company of Giants, *1997*

....

Great Ideas

Ultimately, it comes down to taste. It comes down to trying to expose yourself to the best things that humans have done and then try to bring those things in to what you're doing. Picasso had a saying: good artists copy, great artists steal. And we have always been shameless about stealing great ideas, and I think part of what made the Macintosh great was that the people working on it were musicians and poets and artists and zoologists and historians who also happened to be the best computer scientists in the world.

—Triumph of the Nerds, *PBS, June 1996*

....

Great Product Design

We ended up opting for these Miele appliances, made in Germany.... These guys really thought the process through. They did such a great job designing these washers and dryers. I got more thrill out of them than I have out of any piece of high tech in years.

—Wired, *February 1996*

Great Products

Actually, making an insanely great product has a lot to do with the process of making the product, how you learn things and adopt new ideas and throw out old ideas.

—Playboy, *February 1985*

You know, my philosophy is—it's always been very simple. And it has its flaws, which I'll go into. My philosophy is that everything starts with a great product. So, you know, I obviously believed in listening to customers, but customers can't tell you about the next breakthrough that's going to happen next year that's going to change the whole industry. So you have to listen very carefully. But then you have to go and sort of stow away—you have to go hide away with people that really understand the technology, but also really care about the customers, and dream up this next breakthrough. And that's my perspective, that everything starts with a great product. And that has its flaws. I have certainly been accused of not listening to the customers enough. And I think there is probably a certain amount of that that's valid.

—Newsweek, *September 29, 1985*

Hard Work

I'd never been so tired in my life. I'd come home at about ten o'clock at night and flop straight into bed, then haul myself out at six the next morning and take a shower and go to work. My wife deserves all the credit for keeping me at it. She supported me and kept the family together with a husband in absentia.

—*CNNMoney*/Fortune, *November 9, 1998*

Health Speculation

As many of you know, I have been losing weight throughout 2008. The reason has been a mystery to me and my doctors. A few weeks ago, I decided that getting to the root cause of this and reversing it needed to become my #1 priority. Fortunately, after further testing, my doctors think they have found the cause—a hormone imbalance that has been robbing me of the proteins my body needs to be healthy. Sophisticated blood tests have confirmed this diagnosis.... So now I've said more than I wanted to say, and all that I am going to say, about this.

—*Apple Website, January 5, 2009*

Health, Taking Time Off for

In order to take myself out of the limelight and focus on my health, and to allow everyone at Apple to focus on delivering extraordinary products, I have decided to take a medical leave of absence until the end of June.

I have asked Tim Cook to be responsible for Apple's day to day operations, and I know he and the rest of the executive management team will do a great job. As CEO, I plan to remain involved in major strategic decisions while I am out. Our board of directors fully supports this plan.

—Apple media advisory to all Apple employees,
January 14, 2009

....

IBM

Welcome, IBM. Seriously.... And congratulations on your first personal computer. Putting real computing power in the hands of the individual is already improving the way people work, think, learn, communicate, and spend their leisure hours. Computer literacy is fast becoming as fundamental a skill as reading or writing.

—Apple print ad in the Wall Street Journal,
August 24, 1981

IBM wants to wipe us off the face of the earth.

—Fortune, *February 20, 1984*

....

iCEO

Some people worry about the word "interim," but they weren't worried about the last CEO, and he wasn't interim.

—Apple Confidential 2.0, *2004*

• •

Impact, in an Address to Apple Employees

We have a major opportunity to influence where Apple is going. As every day passes, the work fifty people are doing here is going to send a giant ripple through the universe. I am really impressed with the quality of our ripple. I know I might be a little hard to get on with, but this is the most fun I've had in my life. I'm having a blast.

—Return to the Little Kingdom, *2009*

• •

Innovation

A lot of companies have chosen to downsize, and maybe that was the right thing for them. We chose a different path. Our belief was that if we kept putting great products in front of customers, they would continue to open their wallets.

—Success, *June 2010*

Innovation distinguishes between a leader and a follower.

—The Innovation Secrets of Steve Jobs, *2011*

On Microsoft: They were able to copy the Mac because the Mac was frozen in time. The Mac didn't change much for the last 10 years. It changed maybe 10 percent. It was a sitting duck. It's amazing that it took Microsoft 10 years to copy something that was a sitting duck. Apple, unfortunately, doesn't deserve too much sympathy. They invested hundreds and hundreds of millions of dollars into R&D, but very little came out. They produced almost no new innovation since the original Mac itself.

So now, the original genes of the Macintosh have populated the earth. Ninety percent in the form of Windows, but nevertheless, there are tens of millions of computers that work like that. And that's great. The question is, what's next? And what's going to keep driving this PC revolution?

—Rolling Stone, *January 17, 2011*

The people who go to see our movies are trusting us with something very important—their time and their imagination. So in order to respect that trust, we have to keep changing; we have to challenge ourselves and try to surprise our audiences with something new every time.

—To Infinity and Beyond! *2007*

....

Insight

I think the artistry is in having an insight into what one sees around them. Generally putting things together in a way no one else has before and finding a way to express that to other people who don't have that insight....

—*Smithsonian Institution Oral and Video Histories,*
April 20, 1995

We had the hardware experience, the industrial design expertise and the software expertise, including iTunes. One of the biggest insights we had was that we decided not to try to manage your music library on the iPod, but to manage it in iTunes. Other companies tried to do everything on the device itself and made it so complicated that it was useless.

—Newsweek, *October 16, 2006*

● ●

Inspiration

As you've pointed out I've helped with more computers in more schools than anybody else in the world and I'm absolutely convinced that is by no means the most important thing. The most important thing is a *person*. A person who incites and feeds your curiosity; and machines cannot do that in the same way that people can.

—*Smithsonian Institution Oral and Video Histories,*
April 20, 1995

● ●

Integration

Apple's the only company left in this industry that designs the whole widget. Hardware, software, developer relations, marketing. It turns out that that, in my opinion, is Apple's greatest strategic advantage. We didn't have a plan, so it looked like this was a tremendous deficit. But with a plan, it's Apple's core strategic advantage, if you believe that there's still room for innovation in this industry, which I do, because Apple can innovate faster than anyone else.

—Time, *October 10, 1999*

....

Interdisciplinary Talents

I've never believed that they're separate. Leonardo da Vinci was a great artist and a great scientist. Michelangelo knew a tremendous amount about how to cut stone at the quarry. The finest dozen computer scientists I know are all musicians. Some are better than others, but they all consider that an important part of their life. I don't believe that the best people in any of these fields see themselves as one branch of a forked tree. I just don't see that. People bring these things together a lot. Dr. Land at Polaroid said, "I want Polaroid to stand at the intersection of art and science," and I've never forgotten that. I think that that's possible, and I think a lot of people have tried.

—Time, *October 10, 1999*

••

Internet Theft and Motivation

We said: We don't see how you can convince people to stop being thieves, unless you can offer them a carrot—not just a stick. And the carrot is: We're gonna offer you a better experience...and it's only gonna cost you a dollar a song.

—Rolling Stone, *June 16, 1994*

None of this technology that you're talking about is gonna work. We have PhDs here that know the stuff cold, and we don't believe it's possible to protect digital content.... What's new is this amazingly efficient distribution system for stolen property called the Internet—and no one's gonna shut down the Internet. And it only takes one stolen copy to be on the Internet. And the way we expressed it to them is: Pick one lock—open any door. It only takes one person to pick a lock.

—Rolling Stone, *June 16, 1994*

••

iPad and Inevitable Change

This transformation's going to make some people uneasy—people from the PC world, like you and me. It's going to make us uneasy because the PC has taken us a long way—it's brilliant. And we like to talk about the post-PC era, but when it really starts to happen, I think it's uncomfortable for a lot of people.

—D8 Conference, June 1–3, 2010

••

iPad Inspires iPhone

I actually started on the tablet first. I had this idea of being able to get rid of the keyboard, type on a multi-touch glass display. And I asked our folks, could we come up with a multi-touch display that I could rest my hands on, and actually type on. And about six months later, they called me in and showed me this prototype display. And it was amazing. This is in the early 2000s. And I gave it to one of our other, really brilliant UI [user interface] folks, and he called me back a few weeks later and he had inertial scrolling working and a few other things. I thought, My God, we could build a phone out of this. And I put the tablet project on the shelf, because the phone was more important. And we took the next several years, and did the iPhone.

—D8 Conference, June 1–3, 2010

· ·

iPhone

iPhone is five years ahead of what everybody else has got. If we didn't do one more thing we'd be set for five years!

—Newsweek, *January 9, 2007*

· ·

iPod Nano

We're in uncharted territory. We've never sold this many of anything before.

—*Apple keynote address, September 12, 2006*

· ·

iPod Touch

Originally, we weren't exactly sure how to market the Touch. Was it an iPhone without the phone? Was it a pocket computer? What happened was, what customers told us was, they started to see it as a game machine. We started to market it that way, and it just took off. And now what we really see is it's the lowest-cost way to the App Store, and that's the big draw. So what we were focused on is just reducing the price to $199. We don't need to add new stuff. We need to get the price down where everyone can afford it.

—New York Times, *September 9, 2009*

iTunes

Napster and Kazaa certainly demonstrated that the Internet was built perfectly for delivering music. The problem is they're illegal. And the services that have sprung up that were legal are pretty anemic in terms of the rights they offer you, and they kind of treat you like a criminal. You can't burn a CD, or you can't put it on your MP3 player. And so our idea was to come up with a music service where you don't have to subscribe to it. You can just buy music at 99 cents a song, and you have great digital—you have great rights to use it. You can burn as many CDs as you want for personal use, you can put it on your iPods, you can use it in your other applications, you can have it on multiple computers.

—*Apple keynote address, September 12, 2006*

••

Jobs's *Curriculum Vitae* (Résumé)

Objective: I'm looking for a fixer-upper with a solid foundation. Am willing to tear down walls, build bridges, and light fires. I have great experience, lots of energy, a bit of that "vision thing" and I'm not afraid to start from the beginning. Skills: That "vision thing," public speaking, motivating teams, and helping to create really amazing products.

—Steve Jobs's résumé, a placeholder ad to promote iTools, on me.com, January 5, 2000

••

Jobs's Legacy at Apple

If Apple becomes a place where computers are a commodity item, where the romance is gone, and where people forget that computers are the most incredible invention that man has ever invented, I'll feel I have lost Apple. But if I'm a million miles away, and all those people still feel those things… then I will feel that my genes are still there.

—Newsweek, *September 29, 1985*

....

Jobs's $1 Annual Salary

I get 50 cents a year for showing up...and the other 50 cents is based on my performance.

—*AppleInsider.com, May 10, 2007*

....

Letting Go of the Past

When I got back here in 1997 I was looking for more room, and I found an archive of old Macs and other stuff. I shipped all that off to Stanford. If you look backward in this business, you'll be crushed. You have to look forward.

—Wired, *December 22, 2008*

....

Life's Complications

It's insane: We all have busy lives, we have jobs, we have interests, and some of us have children. Everyone's lives are just getting busier, not less busy, in this busy society. You just don't have time to learn this stuff, and everything's getting more complicated.... We both don't have a lot of time to learn how to use a washing machine or a phone.

—The Independent, *October 29, 2005*

. . . .

Losing Market Share

And how are monopolies lost? Think about it.
Some very good product people invent some
very good products, and the company achieves
a monopoly. But after that, the product people
aren't the ones that drive the company forward
anymore. It's the marketing guys or the ones
who expand the business into Latin America or
whatever.... So a different group of people start to
move up. And who usually ends up running the
show? The sales guy.

—Bloomberg Businessweek, *October 12, 2004*

. . . .

Losing Money

I'm the only person I know that's lost a quarter of
a billion dollars in one year.... It's very character-
building.

—Apple Confidential 2.0, *2004*

· ·

Lost Opportunities

So we went to Atari and said, "Hey, we've got this amazing thing, even built with some of your parts, and what do you think about funding us? Or we'll give it to you. We just want to do it. Pay our salary, we'll come work for you." And they said, "No." So then we went to Hewlett-Packard, and they said, "Hey, we don't need you. You haven't got through college yet.'"

—Fast Company, *August 11, 2009*

· ·

Mac Cube

Ahead of its time, a commercial bust: The G4 Cube is simply the coolest computer ever. An entirely new class of computer, it marries the Pentium-crushing performance of the Power Mac G4 with the miniaturization, silent operation and elegant desktop design of the iMac. It is an amazing engineering and design feat, and we're thrilled to finally unveil it to our customers.

—*Macworld Expo, 2000*

Mac's Introduction

It is now 1984. It appears IBM wants it all. Apple is perceived to be the only hope to offer IBM a run for its money. Dealers initially welcoming IBM with open arms now fear an IBM dominated and controlled future. They are increasingly turning back to Apple as the only force that can ensure their future freedom. IBM wants it all, and is aiming its guns on its last obstacle to industry control: Apple. Will "Big Blue" dominate the entire computer industry? The entire information age? Was George Orwell right?

—Apple special event for the Macintosh, January 1984

Mac Legacy

You saw the 1984 commercial. Macintosh was basically this relatively small company in Cupertino, California, taking on the goliath, IBM, and saying "Wait a minute, your way is wrong. This is not the way we want computers to go. This is not the legacy we want to leave. This is not what we want our kids to be learning. This is wrong and we are going to show you the right way to do it and here it is. It's called Macintosh and it is so much better."

—Smithsonian Institution Oral and Video Histories,
April 20, 1995

●●●

Making Bold Announcements

I understand the appeal of a slow burn, but personally I'm a big-bang guy.

—*Harvard Business School*, Working Knowledge for
Business Leaders, *June 16, 2003*

●●●

Marketing

My dream is that every person in the world will have their own Apple computer. To do that, we've got to be a great marketing company.

—Odyssey: Pepsi to Apple, *1987*

· ·

Microsoft's Lack of Innovation

The only problem with Microsoft is they just have no taste. I don't mean that in a small way. I mean that in a big way, in the sense that they don't think of original ideas and they don't bring much culture into their products. I have no problem with their success—they've earned their success for the most part. I have a problem with the fact that they just make really third-rate products

—Triumph of the Nerds, *PBS, June 1996*

The thing I don't think is good is that I don't believe Microsoft has transformed itself into an agent for improving things, an agent for coming up with the next revolution. The Japanese, for example, used to be accused of just copying—and indeed, in the beginning, that's just what they did. But they got quite a bit more sophisticated and started to innovate—look at automobiles, they certainly innovated quite a bit there. I can't say the same thing about Microsoft.

—Rolling Stone, *January 17, 2011*

••

Microsoft's Microview

I told [Bill Gates] I believed every word of what I said but that I should never have said it in public. I wish him the best, I really do. I just think he and Microsoft are a bit narrow. He'd be a broader guy if he had dropped acid once or gone off to an ashram when he was younger.

—New York Times Magazine, *January 12, 1997*

••

Misplaced Values

You know, my main reaction to this money thing is that it's humorous, all the attention to it, because it's hardly the most insightful or valuable thing that's happened to me in the past ten years. But it makes me feel old, sometimes, when I speak at a campus and I find that what students are most in awe of is the fact that I'm a millionaire.

—Playboy, *February 1985*

●●●

Mistakes

On dropping Flash on Apple products: Some things are good in a product, some things are bad. If the market tells us we're making bad choices, we'll make changes.

—*D8 conference, June 1, 2010*

●●●

Money

Innovation has nothing to do with how many R&D dollars you have. When Apple came up with the Mac, IBM was spending at least 100 times more on R&D. It's not about money. It's about the people you have, how you're led, and how much you get it.... Rarely do I find an important product or service in people's lives where you don't have at least two competitors. Apple is positioned beautifully to be that second competitor.

—*CNNMoney/*Fortune, *November 9, 1998*

I was worth about over a million dollars when I was twenty-three and over ten million dollars when I was twenty-four, and over a hundred million dollars when I was twenty-five, and it wasn't important because I never did it for the money.

—Triumph of the Nerds, *PBS, June 1996*

· ·

Motivating Employees

What happens in most companies is that you don't keep great people under working environments where individual accomplishment is discouraged rather than encouraged. The great people leave and you end up with mediocrity. I know, because that's how Apple was built.

—Playboy, *February 1985*

The people who are doing the work are the moving force behind the Macintosh. My job is to create a space for them, to clear out the rest of the organization and keep it at bay.... This is the neatest group of people I've ever worked with. They're all exceptionally bright, but more importantly they share a quality about the way they look at life, which is that the journey is the reward. They really want to see this product out in the world. It's more important than their personal lives right now.

—Macworld, *no. 1, February 1984*

Motivation

To former PepsiCo executive John Sculley, whom Jobs was trying to woo to Apple: Do you want to spend the rest of your life selling sugared water, or do you want a chance to change the world?

—Odyssey: Pepsi to Apple, *1987*

It's better to be a pirate than to join the Navy.

—Odyssey: Pepsi to Apple, *1987*

••

Need for Teamwork

In our business, one person can't do anything anymore. You create a team of people around you. You have a responsibility of integrity of work to that team. Everybody does try to turn out the best work that they can.

—Smithsonian Institution Oral and Video Histories,
April 20, 1995

••

Netbooks

Netbooks aren't better than anything. They're just cheap laptops.

—Apple event for iPad 1, January 27, 2010

New Products

I've said this before, but thought it was worth repeating: It's in Apple's DNA that technology alone is not enough. That it's technology married with liberal arts, married with the humanities, that yields us the result that makes our hearts sing. And nowhere is that more true than in these post-PC devices.

And a lot of folks in this tablet market are rushing in and they're looking at this as the next PC. The hardware and the software are done by different companies. And they're talking about speeds and feeds just like they did with PCs.

And our experience and every bone in our body says that that is not the right approach to this. That these are post-PC devices that need to be even easier to use than a PC. That need to be even more intuitive than a PC. And where the software and the hardware and the applications need to intertwine in an even more seamless way than they do on a PC.

And we think we're on the right track with this. We think we have the right architecture not just in silicon, but in the organization to build these kinds of products.

And so I think we stand a pretty good chance of being pretty competitive in this market. And I hope that what you've seen today gives you a good feel for that.

—Apple event for iPad 2, March 2, 2011

• •

No Resting on Laurels

I think if you do something and it turns out pretty good, then you should go do something else wonderful, not dwell on it for too long. Just figure out what's next.

—msnbc.com, May 25, 2006

• •

Owning the User Experience

We're the only company that owns the whole widget—the hardware, the software and the operating system. We can take full responsibility for the user experience. We can do things the other guy can't do.

—Time, January 14, 2002

. . . .

Packaging

It was clear to me that for every hardware hobbyist who wanted to assemble his own computer, there were a thousand people who couldn't do that but wanted to mess around with programming...just like I did when I was 10. My dream for the Apple II was to sell the first real packaged computer...I got a bug up my rear that I wanted the computer in a plastic case.

—*AppleDesign, 1997*

. . . .

PARC's Graphical Interface

The Alto has the world's first graphical user interface. It had windows. It had a crude menu system. It had crude panels and stuff. It didn't work right but it basically was all there.... I was so blown away with the potential of the germ of that graphical user interface that I saw that I didn't even assimilate or even stick around to investigate fully the other two.

—*Smithsonian Institution Oral and Video Histories, April 20, 1995*

••

PARC's Innovations

[Xerox's Palo Alto Research Center] didn't have
it totally right, but they had the germ of the idea
of all three things. And the three things were:
graphical user interfaces, object-oriented computing, and networking.

—*Smithsonian Institution Oral and Video Histories,*
April 20, 1995

••

Parochial Thinking

Music companies make more money when they
sell a song on iTunes than when they sell a CD.
If they want to raise prices, it's because they're
greedy. If the price goes up, people turn back to
piracy—and everybody loses.

—Guardian, *September 22, 2005*

Partnership

We don't think one company can do everything. So you've got to partner with people that are really good at stuff.... We're not trying to be great at search, so we partner with people who are great at search.... We know how to do the best map clients in the world, but we don't know how to do the back end, so we partner with people that know how to do the back end. And what we want to do is be that consumer's device and that consumer's experience wrapped around all this information and things we can deliver to them in a wonderful user interface, in a coherent product.

—*D5 Conference: All Things Digital, May 30, 2007*

Passion

People say you have to have a lot of passion for
what you're doing and it's totally true. And the
reason is because it's so hard that if you don't, any
rational person would give up. It's really hard.
And you have to do it over a sustained period of
time. So if you don't love it, if you're not having
fun doing it, you don't really love it, you're going to
give up. And that's what happens to most people,
actually. If you really look at the ones that ended
up being "successful" in the eyes of the society
and the ones that didn't, oftentimes it's the ones
[who] were successful loved what they did, so they
could persevere when it got really tough. And the
ones that didn't love it quit because they're sane,
right? Who would want to put up with this stuff if
you don't love it? So it's a lot of hard work and it's
a lot of worrying constantly and if you don't love
it, you're going to fail.

—*D5 Conference: All Things Digital, May 30, 2007*

You've got to find what you love. And that is as
true for your work as it is for your lovers. Your
work is going to fill a large part of your life, and
the only way to be truly satisfied is to do what you
believe is great work. And the only way to do great
work is to love what you do…. Don't settle.

—*Commencement address, Stanford University,*
June 12, 2005

· ·

Passive versus Active Thinking

We don't think that televisions and personal computers are going to merge. We think basically you watch television to turn your brain off, and you work on your computer when you want to turn your brain on.

—Macworld, *February 2, 2004*

· ·

PC as the Digital Hub

We believe the next great era is for the personal computer to be the digital hub of all these devices.

—Time, *January 14, 2002*

· ·

Perception

One of the reasons I think Microsoft took ten years to copy the Mac is 'cause they didn't really get it at its core.

—Rolling Stone, *June 16, 1994*

....

Perseverance

I'm convinced that about half of what separates
the successful entrepreneurs from the non-suc-
cessful ones is pure perseverance.... Unless you
have a lot of passion about this, you're not going
to survive. You're going to give it up. So you've got
to have an idea, or a problem or a wrong that you
want to right that you're passionate about; otherwise, you're not going to have the perseverance to
stick it through.

—Smithsonian Institution Oral and Video Histories,
April 20, 1995

....

Pixar

Pixar's got by far and away the best computer
graphics talent in the entire world, and it now has
the best animation and artistic talent in the whole
world to do these kinds of film. There's really no
one else in the world who could do this stuff. It's
really phenomenal. We're probably close to ten
years ahead of anybody else.

—Smithsonian Institution Oral and Video Histories,
April 20, 1995

We believe [*Toy Story*] is the biggest advance in animation since Walt Disney started it all with the release of *Snow White* 50 years ago.

—*CNNMoney*/Fortune, *September 18, 1995*

••

Pixar's People

Apple has some pretty amazing people, but the collection of people at Pixar is the highest concentration of remarkable people I have ever witnessed. There's a person who's got a Ph.D. in computer-generated plants—3-D grass and trees and flowers. There's another who is the best in the world at putting imagery on film. Also, Pixar is more multidisciplinary than Apple ever will be. But the key thing is that it is much smaller. Pixar's got 450 people. You could never have the collection of people that Pixar has now if you went to two thousand people.

—*CNNMoney*/Fortune, *November 9, 1998*

. . . .

Porn Apps on Android

There's a porn store for Android that you can go to, and it's got nothing but porn apps for your Android phone. And you can download them, and your kids can download them, and your kids' friends can download them on their phones. And that's just not the place where we want to go.

—Apple event for iPhone 4.0 software, April 8, 2010

. . . .

Pride in Product

On the 47 Mac team members who signed the plastic mold casing for the first Macintosh: Artists sign their work.

—Folklore.org, February 1982

••

Priorities Assessment

On meeting his wife, Laurene: I was in the parking lot, with the key in the car, and I thought to myself: If this is my last night on earth, would I rather spend it at a business meeting or with this woman? I ran across the parking lot, asked her if she'd have dinner with me. She said yes, we walked into town, and we've been together ever since.

—New York Times Magazine, *January 12, 1997*

••

Process

The system is that there is no system. That doesn't mean we don't have process. Apple is a very disciplined company, and we have great processes. But that's not what it's about. Process makes you more efficient.

—Bloomberg Businessweek, *October 12, 2004*

••

Products

Jim McCluney, former head of Apple's worldwide operations, recalls Jobs's criticisms voiced to key Apple executives in July 1997, after Gil Amelio resigned and Jobs assumed control: It's the products. The products SUCK! There's no sex in them anymore!

—Bloomberg Businessweek, *February 6, 2006*

••

Product Creation

When we create stuff, we do it because we listen to customers, get their inputs and also throw in what we'd like to see, too. We cook up new products. You never really know if people will love them as much as you do.

—*CNBC.com, September 5, 2007*

••

Product Design

Regarding OS X's Aqua user interface: We made the buttons on the screen look so good, you'll want to lick them.

—*CNNMoney/*Fortune, *2000*

Product Imagination

It's not about pop culture, and it's not about fooling people, and it's not about convincing people that they want something they don't. We figure out what we want. And I think we're pretty good at having the right discipline to think through whether a lot of other people are going to want it, too. That's what we get paid to do. So you can't go out and ask people, you know, what's the next big [thing]? There's a great quote by Henry Ford who said, "If I'd have asked my customers what they wanted, they would have told me 'A faster horse.'"

—*CNNMoney/*Fortune, *February 2008*

Product Innovation

What Apple has always stood for is product innovation. Apple invented this industry with the Apple II and I think the Mac has provided the innovation that much of the industry has been living off of for the last 10 years. And it's time for someone to come up with some new innovation to drive the industry forward, and who better to do that than Apple.

—*CNN.com, April 23, 2004*

....

Product Integration

The things I'm most proud about at Apple is [sic] where the technical and the humanistic come together, as it did in publishing. The typographic artistry coupled with the technical understanding and excellence to implement that electronically came together and empowered people to use the computer without having to understand arcane computer commands. It was the combination of those two things that I'm the most proud of.

—Smithsonian Institution Oral and Video Histories,
April 20, 1995

Apple has a core set of talents, and those talents are: We do, I think, very good hardware design; we do very good industrial design; and we write very good system and application software. And we're really good at packaging that all together into a product. We're the only people left in the computer industry that do that.

—Rolling Stone, *June 16, 1994*

Apple is the most creative technology company out there—just like Pixar is the most technologically adept creative company.... Also, almost all recording artists use Macs and they have iPods, and now most of the music industry people have iPods as well. There's a trust in the music community that Apple will do something right—that it won't cut corners—and that it cares about the creative process and about the music. Also, our solution encompasses operating system software, server software, application software, and hardware. Apple is the only company in the world that has all that under one roof. We can invent a complete solution that works—and take responsibility for it.

—Bloomberg Businessweek, *February 2, 2004*

One company makes the software. The other makes the hardware...It's not working. The innovation can't happen fast enough. The integration isn't seamless enough. No one takes responsibility for the user interface. It's a mess.

—Time, *October 16, 2005*

· ·

Product Secrecy

We never talk about future products. There used to be a saying at Apple: Isn't it funny? A ship that leaks from the top. So—I don't wanna perpetuate that. So I really can't say.

—ABCNews.com, June 29, 2005

· ·

Products' Appeal

The products speak for themselves.

—Playboy, *February 1985*

· ·

Profit Sharing, Not Advances

The remedy is to stop paying advances. The remedy is to go to a gross-revenues deal and to tell an artist: We'll give you 20 cents on every dollar we get…but we're not gonna give you an advance. The accounting will be simple: The more successful you are, the more you'll earn. But if you're not successful, you will not earn a dime. We'll go ahead and risk some marketing money on you, and we'll be out. But if you're not successful, you'll make no money—but if you are, you'll make a lot more. That's the way out. That's the way the rest of the world works.

—Rolling Stone, *December 3, 2003*

Quality

We just wanted to build the best thing we could build. When you're a carpenter making a beautiful chest of drawers, you're not going to use a piece of plywood on the back, even though it faces the wall and nobody will ever see it. You'll know it's there, so you're going to use a beautiful piece of wood on the back. For you to sleep well at night, the aesthetic, the quality, has to be carried all the way through.

—Playboy, *February 1985*

Quality is more important than quantity. One home run is much better than two doubles.

—Bloomberg Businessweek, *February 6, 2006*

Real Estate Location

On the location of Apple stores in high-end malls: The real estate was a lot more expensive [but people] didn't have to gamble with 20 minutes of their time. They only had to gamble with 20 foot-steps of their time.

—*CNNMoney*/Fortune, *March 8, 2007*

··

Reliability

It just works.

—Frequently used phrase at Apple events

··

Repeating Success

There's a classic thing in business, which is the second-product syndrome. Often companies that have a really successful first product don't quite understand why that product was so successful. And so with the second product, their ambitions grow and they get much more grandiose, and their second product fails. They fail to get it out, or it fails to resonate with the marketplace because they really didn't understand why their first product resonated with the marketplace.

—To Infinity and Beyond! 2007

Risking Failure

One of my role models is Bob Dylan. As I grew up, I learned the lyrics to all his songs and watched him never stand still. If you look at the artists, if they get really good, it always occurs to them at some point that they can do this one thing for the rest of their lives, and they can be really successful to the outside world but not really be successful to themselves. That's the moment that an artist really decides who he or she is. If they keep on risking failure, they're still artists. Dylan and Picasso were always risking failure.

This Apple thing is that way for me. I don't want to fail, of course. But even though I didn't know how bad things really were, I still had a lot to think about before I said *yes*. I had to consider the implications for Pixar, for my family, for my reputation. I decided that I didn't really care, because this is what I want to do. If I try my best and fail, well, I've tried my best.

—*CNNMoney*/Fortune, *November 9, 1998*

• •

Shared Vision

The thing that bound us together at Apple was the ability to make things that were going to change the world. That was very important.

—Smithsonian Institution Oral and Video Histories,
April 20, 1995

• •

Simplicity

As technology becomes more complex, Apple's core strength of knowing how to make very so-phisticated technology comprehensible to mere mortals is in even greater demand. The Dells of the world don't spend money; they don't think about these things.

—New York Times Magazine, *November 30, 2003*

If we could make four great product platforms that's all we need. We can put our A team on every single one of them instead of having a B or a C team on any. We can turn them much faster.

—Keynote address, Seybold Seminars, March 1998

There's a very strong DNA within Apple, and that's about taking state-of-the-art technology and making it easy for people...people who don't want to read manuals, people who live very busy lives.

—Guardian, *September 22, 2005*

Regarding the simplicity of the iMac: If you go out and ask people what's wrong with computers today, they'll tell you they're really complicated, they have a zillion cables coming out of the back, they're really big and noisy, they're really ugly, and they take forever to get on the Internet. And so we tried to set out to fix those problems with products like the iMac. I mean, the iMac is the only desktop computer that comes in only one box. You can set it up and be surfing the Internet in 15 minutes or less.

—*Macworld Expo, March 13, 1999*

We've reviewed the road map of new products and axed more than 70 percent of them, keeping the 30 percent that were gems. The product teams at Apple are very excited. There's so much low-hanging fruit, it's easy to turn around.

—*Macworld Expo, January 6, 1998*

Mobile devices are really important to people. It's not like this is an obscure product category that affects just a small part of the population. People have seen in the demos and our ads something they instantly know they can figure out how to use. People throw technology at us constantly, and most of us say "I don't have time to figure that out." Most of us have experiences with our current mobile phones and can't figure them out.

—USA Today, *July 28, 2007*

....

Slogan: First Generation iPod

One thousand songs in your pocket.

—*Apple advertisement, October 31, 2001*

....

Software

Bill [Gates] built the first software company in the industry. And I think he built the first software company before anyone in our industry knew what a software company was, and that was huge. And the business model they ended up pursuing ended up working real well. Bill was focused on software before anyone else had a clue. There's a lot more you can say, but that's the high-order bit.

—*D5 Conference: All Things Digital, May 30, 2007*

What's really interesting is if you look at the reason that the iPod exists and that Apple's in that marketplace, it's because these really great Japanese consumer electronic companies who kind of own the portable music market, invented it and owned it, couldn't do the appropriate software, couldn't conceive of and implement the appropriate software. Because an iPod's really just software. It's software in the iPod itself, it's software on the PC or the Mac, and it's software in the cloud for the store.

—*D5 Conference: All Things Digital, May 30, 2007*

Re: iMovie software—It makes your camcorder worth ten times as much because you can convert raw footage into an incredible movie with transitions, cross dissolves, credits, soundtracks. You can convert raw footage that you'd normally never look at again on your camcorder into an incredibly emotional piece of communication. Professional. Personal. It's amazing...it has ten times as much value to you.

—*Keynote speech at Macworld, January 9, 2001*

••

Soul of the New Machine

You know, if the hardware is the brain and the sinew of our products, the software in them is their soul.

—*Keynote address, Apple Worldwide Development Conference, June 6–10, 2011*

••

Stagnation, the Danger of

On Apple during his decade-long absence: The trouble with Apple is it succeeded beyond its wildest dreams. We succeeded so well, we got everyone else to dream the same dream. The rest of the world became just like it. The trouble is, the dream didn't evolve. Apple stopped creating.

—Apple Confidential 2.0, *2004*

••

Stickiness

You don't need to take notes. If it's important, you'll remember it.

—Inside Steve's Brain, *2009*

· ·

Stock Options

At Apple we gave all our employees stock options very early on. We were among the first in Silicon Valley to do that. And when I returned, I took away most of the cash bonuses and replaced them with options. No cars, no planes, no bonuses. Basically, everybody gets a salary and stock.... It's a very egalitarian way to run a company that Hewlett-Packard pioneered and that Apple, I would like to think, helped establish.

—*CNNMoney/*Fortune, *November 9, 1998*

· ·

Story, Importance of

We've pioneered the whole medium of computer animation, but John [Lasseter] once said—and this really stuck with me—"No amount of technology will turn a bad story into a good story."... That dedication to quality is really ingrained in the culture of this studio.

—To Infinity and Beyond! *2007*

....

Strategy

After departing Apple: You know, I've got a plan that could rescue Apple. I can't say any more than that it's the perfect product and the perfect strategy for Apple. But nobody there will listen to me.

—*CNNMoney*/Fortune, *September 18, 1995*

....

Success

Pixar's seen by a lot of folks as an overnight success, but if you really look closely, most overnight successes took a long time.

—To Infinity and Beyond! *2007*

....

Sucker-Punched, Being

I feel like somebody just punched me in the stomach and knocked all my wind out. I'm only 30 years old and I want to have a chance to continue creating things. I know I've got at least one more great computer in me. And Apple is not going to give me a chance to do that.

—Playboy, *February 1985*

. . . .

Survival

Victory in our industry is spelled *survival.* The way we're going to survive is to innovate our way out of this.

—Time, *February 5, 2003*

. . . .

Takeovers, Hostile

On a planned takeover engineered by Oracle's Larry Ellison, restoring Jobs as the head of Apple: I decided I'm not a hostile-takeover kind of guy. If they had [asked] me to come back, it might have been different.

—Time, *February 5, 2003*

. . . .

Taking Stock of Apple

On his single share of Apple stock: Yes, I sold the shares. I pretty much had given up hope that the Apple board was going to do anything. I didn't think the stock was going up. [*After Jobs's departure, Apple stock reached its lowest level ever.*]

—Time, *August 18, 1997*

....

Teamwork

My model for business is the Beatles. They were four guys who kept each other's kind of negative tendencies in check. They balanced each other and the total was greater than the sum of the parts. That's how I see business: great things in business are never done by one person, they're done by a team of people.

—60 Minutes, *2003*

....

Technology in Perspective

[Technology] doesn't change the world. It really doesn't. Technologies can make it easier, can let us touch people we might not otherwise. But it's a disservice to constantly put things in a radical new light, that it's going to change everything. Things don't have to change the world to be important.

—The Independent, *October 29, 2005*

"Think Different" Ad Campaign

Well, I gotta tell you—we don't do it because it goes down well or not. We have a problem, and our problem was that people had forgotten what Apple stands for. As a matter of fact, a lot of our employees have forgotten what Apple stands for. And so we needed a way to communicate what the heck Apple's all about. And we thought, how do you tell somebody what you are, who you are, what you care about? And the best way we could think of was, you know, if you know who somebody's heroes are, that tells you a lot about them. So we thought we're going to tell people who our heroes are, and that's what the "Think Different" campaign is about. It's about telling people who we admire, who we think are the heroes of this century. And—some people will like us, and some people won't like us.

— *Macworld Expo, March 13, 1999*

•••

Thinking Through the Problem

Once you get into the problem…you see that it's complicated, and you come up with all these con-voluted solutions. That's where most people stop, and the solutions tend to work for a while. But the really great person will keep going, find the underlying problem, and come up with an elegant solution that works on every level. That's what we wanted to do with the Mac.

—AppleDesign, *1997*

We have a lot of customers, and we have a lot of research into our installed base. We also watch industry trends pretty carefully. But in the end, for something this complicated, it's really hard to design products by focus groups. A lot of times, people don't know what they want until you show it to them.

—Bloomberg Businessweek, *May 25, 1998*

. . . .

To Be or Not to Be

Your time is limited, so don't waste it living some-one else's life. Don't be trapped by dogma—which is living with the results of other people's think-ing. Don't let the noise of others' opinions drown our your own inner voice. And most important, have the courage to follow your heart and intui-tion. They somehow already know what you truly want to become. Everything else is secondary.

—Commencement address, Stanford University,
June 12, 2005

. . . .

Toy Story 2

On how Pixar's commitment to Toy Story 2 *ex-acted a heavy toll on the company's employees:* Everybody was so dedicated to it and loved *Toy Story* and those characters so much, and loved the new movie so much, that we killed ourselves to make it. It took some people a year to recover. It was tough—it was too tough, but we did it. Now enough time has passed that we can look back on that and we're glad we did it. But it was tough.

—To Infinity and Beyond! 2007

· ·

Trash Talking

Adam Osborne is always dumping on Apple. He was going on and on about Lisa, and when we would ship Lisa, and then he started joking about Mac. I was trying to keep my cool and be polite but he kept asking, "What's this Mac we're hearing about? Is it real?" He started getting under my collar so much that I told him, "Adam, it's so good that even after it puts your company out of business, you'll *still* want to go out and buy it for your kids."

—Apple Confidential 2.0, *2004*

· ·

Ubiquity of Mac

Apple's in a pretty interesting position. Because, as you may know, almost every song and CD is made on a Mac—it's recorded on a Mac; it's mixed on a Mac. The artwork's done on a Mac. Almost every artist I've met has an iPod, and most of the music execs now have iPods.

—Rolling Stone, *December 3, 2003*

••

User Experience

At Apple we come at everything asking, "How easy is this going to be for the user? How great it is going to be for the user?" After that, it's like at Pixar. Everyone in Hollywood says the key to good animated movies is story, story, story. But when it really gets down to it, when the story isn't working, they will not stop production and spend more money and get the story right. That's what I see about the software business. Everybody says, "Oh, the user is the most important thing," but nobody else really does it.

—*CNNMoney*/Fortune, *February 21, 2005*

••

Values

On Zen Buddhism: It places value on experience versus intellectual understanding. I saw a lot of people contemplating things but it didn't seem to lead to too many places. I got very interested in people who had discovered something more significant than an intellectual, abstract understanding.

—Return to the Little Kingdom, *2009*

· ·

Vision

We're gambling on our vision, and we would rather do that than make "me, too" products. Let some other companies do that. For us, it's always the next dream.

—Apple product event for the first Macintosh
computer, January 24, 1984

I'm always keeping my eyes open for the next big opportunity, but the way the world is now, it will take enormous resources, both in money and in engineering talent, to make it happen. I don't know what that next big thing might be, but I have a few ideas.

*—CNNMoney/*Fortune, *January 24, 2001*

· ·

Wisdom

I would trade all my technology for an afternoon with Socrates.

—Newsweek, October 28, 2001

....

Working Hard and Growing Older

I read something Bill Gates said about six months ago. He said, "I worked really, really hard in my twenties." And I know what he means, because I worked really, really hard in my twenties, too—seven days a week, lots of hours every day. But you can't do it forever. You don't want to do it forever.

—Time, *October 10, 1999*

....

Zen

The heaviness of being successful was replaced by the lightness of being a beginner again, less sure about everything. It freed me to enter one of the most creative periods of my life. [*An allusion to a popular saying by Zen master Shunryu Suzuki: "In the beginner's mind there are many possibilities, but in the expert's there are few."*]

—*Commencement address, Stanford University, June 12, 2005*

MILESTONES

1955

SJ born in San Francisco to Abdulfattah "John" Jandali and Joanne Simpson. He is given up for adoption to Paul and Clara Jobs, who name him Steven Paul Jobs. (February 24)

1966

The Jobs family moves to Los Altos, California, and SJ enters Homestead High School, where he develops an interest in music (especially Bob Dylan and the Beatles) and electronics.

1969

SJ (age 14) meets future Apple cofounder Stephen "Woz" Wozniak (age 19), both students at Homestead High School.

1972

SJ and Wozniak build and sell illegal tone generators called "blue boxes" to college students who use them to make free phone calls. (An October 1971 article in *Esquire* explained how to make them.) They illicitly earn $6,000 before moving on to legitimate ventures.

SJ graduates from high school. He enrolls in Reed College (Portland, Oregon) in September, but drops out after one semester, though he continues to audit classes while living a bohemian lifestyle.

At Reed, SJ meets future Apple employee Dan Kottke, who would later go on to assemble and test the first Apple I computer.

1974

SJ takes a job at Nolan Bushnell's video game company, Atari. (September)

SJ begins attending the Homebrew Computer Club, composed of electronics hobbyists.

1976

Apple is cofounded by SJ (45% share), Wozniak (45% share), and Ronald Wayne (10% share). Wayne decides he can't take the risk and sells his 10% share of Apple back to SJ and Woz for $800. (April 1)

Apple Computer moves to Stevens Creek Boulevard in Cupertino, California, its first office building.

SJ gets an order for 50 computers from the Byte Shop in Mountain View, California. The owner is expecting turnkey computers, but Apple delivers only the heart of the computer, the circuit board. SJ expected computer hobbyists to add the requisite peripherals themselves: a keyboard, a monitor (a CRT television set), a power supply, and a case. (April)

SJ and Kottke exhibit the Apple I at the Personal Computer Festival in Atlantic City, New Jersey. Meanwhile, Wozniak works on Apple II, a major leap forward—a mass market, ready-to-use-out-of-the-box personal computer. (August)

1977

Apple debuts the Apple II at the West Coast Computer Faire in San Francisco. (April 17)

Apple ships its first Apple II system. (June)

1978

Apple shows its first floppy disk drive for the Apple II at the Consumer Electronics Show (CES) in Las Vegas. (January)

In exchange for a one-third interest in Apple, Mike Markkula, a venture capitalist, invests $91,000 in Apple Computer and also establishes a line of credit for the fledgling company for $250,000 with Bank of America.

Apple begins work on Apple III, its next product for the consumer market, as SJ focuses on creating the first Lisa computer for the business market.

Apple recruits Mike Scott from National Semiconductor to serve as its CEO.

SJ has his first child, Lisa Brennan-Jobs, with then-girlfriend Chrisann Brennan. He assumes no role in raising her, and refuses to accept paternity until a court-ordered test proves high probability for a DNA match.

1979

Apple earns $47 million in revenues.

SJ and other key staffers from Apple visit Xerox PARC (Palo Alto Research Center), where they are exposed to new computer technologies, including the mouse and the graphical user interface (GUI). It is a fortuitous event for SJ, who immediately grasps their implications for the future of computers.

Apple debuts Apple II Plus. (June)

VisiCalc, an electronic spreadsheet program, is released for the Apple II, which helps spur sales of the computer. (October 17)

1980

The Apple IPO sells 4.6 million shares. Initially priced at $22 per share, the stock closes at $29. Apple's valuation: $1.778 billion. (December 12)

1981

Apple debuts the Apple III; its design flaws result in a recall of its first 14,000 units.

Andy Hertzfeld of Apple begins work on the Macintosh, an affordable alternative to SJ's expensive Lisa computer.

On a day dubbed "Black Wednesday" by Apple employees, Apple's CEO Mike Scott, without seeking management approval from the board of directors, fires half of the Apple II team. In turn, the board fires Scott, appoints Markkula as interim CEO, and begins a search for a new CEO. (February 25)

SJ becomes chairman of the board. Markkula becomes president, replacing Scott. (March)

IBM introduces its personal computer, the IBM PC 5150, which SJ publicly derides as technologically inferior; SJ underestimates its appeal, especially to the business community, which overwhelmingly buys it in favor of Apple's products. (August)

1982

Microsoft signs a deal to develop three much-needed applications for the Mac: a spreadsheet, a database, and a business graphics program. (January 22)

SJ appears on *Time* magazine for its cover story, "America's Risk Takers: Steven Jobs of Apple Computer." (February 15)

SJ buys an apartment in New York City that occupies the top two floors of the north tower of the iconic San Remo building. After extensive renovations by architect I.M. Pei, SJ never moves in, and later sells it.

Time overlooks SJ for "Man of the Year" in favor of his creation, dubbing the personal computer as "machine of the year." (December)

1983

SJ goes to New York City to give the media a first look at its powerful business computer, Lisa. While there, he meets, and is favorably impressed with, PepsiCo executive John Sculley, whom he eventually woos to Apple. (January)

Apple officially releases the Lisa (Local Integrated Software Architecture) computer. (January 19)

Apple debuts the Apple IIe, and retires the Apple II Plus computer.

Apple hires Sculley as its CEO. (April 8)

1984

Apple debuts the first Macintosh computer, launching with a groundbreaking TV commercial airing during Super Bowl XVIII. Called "1984," and directed by Ridley Scott, it cost $1.2 million to produce and air. The "Mac" is the world's first mass-market GUI (graphical user interface) computer. (January 22)

Lisa debuts. (January 14)

SJ purchases Jackling House, a 17,000-square-foot mansion in Woodside, California.

Apple buys all 39 pages of available advertising space in *Newsweek*'s "Election Extra" issue in order to promote the Macintosh. (November–December)

SJ and Wozniak are awarded the National Medal of Technology by President Ronald Reagan.

1985

The LaserWriter printer debuts, speeding the explosion in desktop publishing. Also, Lisa is repositioned as the Macintosh XL, but its sales do not improve. (January 23)

Wozniak, unhappy with his largely symbolic role at Apple, resigns to found his own company, where he can concentrate on his first love: inventing electronic products. (February 6)

Macintosh XL is discontinued. (April 29)

Sculley, with the approval of the Apple board of directors, relieves SJ as the head of the Mac division. (In a 2010 interview with Leander Kahney, Sculley graciously acknowledged his mistake in not retaining Jobs: "It's so obvious looking back now that that would have been the right thing to do. We didn't do it, so I blame myself for that one. It would have saved Apple this near-death experience they had.") (May 28)

Feeling betrayed, and lacking confidence in the future of Apple, SJ keeps one share of Apple stock and sells the rest for $70.5 million.

Xerox PARC's Alan Kay, a noted computer visionary, tells SJ that George Lucas is looking to sell Pixar. SJ is interested, but not at the $30 million asking price.

Apple lays off 1,200 employees. (June 14)

SJ goes to Apple's board to announce he's leaving to start a new computer company, NeXT. Apple encourages him, and even offers to be an investment partner. (September 13)

1986

Sculley takes over as Apple's chairman of the board. (January)

Apple retires the original Macintosh and replaces it with the Macintosh 512K Enhanced. (April)

SJ buys The Graphics Group (later named Pixar Animation Studios) from George Lucas for $10 million. SJ becomes its CEO and majority shareholder.

Pixar debuts its graphics workstation, the Pixar Image Computer.

1987

Apple announces the Macintosh SE, and its first color graphics computer, Macintosh II. (March 2)

Apple ships Macintosh II. (November)

1988

The NeXT computer debuts. (October 12)

Pixar introduces the second iteration of the Pixar Image Computer.

1989

Pixar's animated film *Tin Toy* wins an Academy Award.

Apple debuts the Macintosh Portable, which weighs 17 pounds. (September)

1990

SJ discontinues development and sales on the Pixar Image Computer and concentrates on developing its software called RenderMan. (April 30)

1991

SJ marries Laurene Powell at a lodge in Yosemite. (March 18)

Pixar's cash burn rate prompts SJ to reorganize the company to ensure its survival. (March)

1992

Fortune magazine adds SJ to its National Business Hall of Fame.

SJ's biological sister, Mona Simpson, publishes a novel titled *The Lost Father*.

At CES in Chicago, Sculley shows a prototype of the Newton, Apple's personal digital assistant. (May)

1993

Sculley debuts the Newton at Macworld. (January)

Failing to meet sales expectations, NeXT closes its doors. (February 11)

Sculley is replaced as Apple CEO by Michael Spindler. (June 7)

Apple announces major layoffs in the works: 2,500 people worldwide. (July)

Newton ships. (August)

Apple discontinues its Apple II computer and peripherals.

1994

Apple debuts its first PowerPC product, a board that it installs in the company's Centris and Quadra lines of Mac computers. (January)

Apple announces it will license its OS (System 7) to other computer manufacturers. Its first customers include Radius and Power Computing.

SJ unsuccessfully tries to sell Pixar. Among the suitors: Microsoft.

1995

Pocahontas and *Toy Story* are previewed at a Disney event in Central Park. The wildly enthusiastic reception for *Toy Story* buoys SJ's spirits. Realizing that Pixar might turn the financial corner, SJ takes charges of Pixar and assumes dual roles as CEO and president. (January)

Disney releases *Toy Story* on Thanksgiving weekend. The film is a hit and goes on to gross $191 million in domestic receipts. (November)

Pixar's IPO makes SJ a billionaire. (November 29)

1996

Spindler is replaced as Apple CEO by Gilbert Amelio. Soon after, Amelio also assumes the position of chairman. (February 2)

SJ is prominently featured in a PBS documentary about Silicon Valley and computers, *Triumph of the Nerds.* (June)

After promising a new OS that it couldn't deliver, Apple seeks a new OS and narrows it down to BeOS (from former Apple executive, Jean-Louis Gassée) and Steve Job's NeXT software. (November)

SJ, in a presentation to Apple's board, convinces it to buy NeXT and its assets for $400 million, with its OS as the major asset. SJ is now back at Apple, albeit in an unofficial advisory capacity. (December)

1997

SJ and Wozniak, after a prolonged absence, return to Macworld Expo to help re-energize Apple. (January)

Amelio announces that Newton may be dropped from the product line.

Newly minted executive committee members SJ and Wozniak become advisors to Amelio. (February)

Amelio resigns. SJ becomes Apple's interim chief executive, which he terms "iCEO," after being offered the CEO position. Citing his continuing interest in Pixar, SJ declines. (July 9)

SJ begins the effort to simplify Apple's product line from four dozen computer models to ten.

At Macworld, SJ announces new deals with former business opponent Microsoft, which is met with mixed feelings by Apple followers. (August)

SJ formally announced as Apple's interim CEO. (John Sculley, in a 2010 interview with Leander Kahney, noted: "I'm actually convinced that if Steve hadn't come back when he did—if they had waited another six months—Apple would have been history. It would have been gone, absolutely gone.") (September)

Apple debuts its Power Mac and PowerBook, which run on the PowerPC G3 chip. (November)

SJ assumes dual CEO responsibilities at Apple and Pixar.

1998

Apple's acquisition of NeXTSTEP lays the foundation for its next major software upgrade: Mac OS X, a Unix-based system.

At Macworld in San Francisco, Apple announces the Power Mac G3 tower unit. (January)

SJ is featured in PBS's documentary, *Nerds 2.0.1: A Brief History of the Internet*, a follow-up to its *Triumph of the Nerds.*

SJ cleans house at Apple: He significantly decreases the number of products in the competing computer lines, kills numerous projects (notably Newton), kills the software-licensing program, and fires select employees. (March)

Pixar releases *A Bug's Life*, which grosses $162 million domestically. (November 20)

1999

Apple announces the candy-colored iMac in five eye-popping colors and new Power Mac G3 tower units. (January 5)

SJ is depicted in a TV docudrama, portrayed by Noah Wyle, called *Pirates of Silicon Valley*. (June 20)

Apple debuts the clam-shelled, portable iBook, a pro laptop called the PowerBook, and its first wireless network device, the Airport base station. (July)

Pixar releases *Toy Story 2*, which grosses $245 million domestically. (October 2)

2000

At Macworld, SJ announces that he's dropped his interim CEO status to become permanent CEO. (January 5)

SJ announces Mac OS X, built on the bones of NeXT's object-oriented software.

Apple ships the iMac. (September 1)

After its lackluster earnings are reported, Apple stock drops to $25 a share. (September 28)

2001

At Macworld, SJ shows Mac OS X, G4 tower computers, and a titanium PowerBook G4 computer. (January 9)

Apple opens its flagship retail store in New York City. (Within ten years, more than 300 such stores opened worldwide.) (May)

The iPod debuts with the ad line, "1,000 songs in your pocket."

Pixar releases *Monsters, Inc.*, which grosses $255 million domestically. (November 2)

2002

Apple introduces the eMac, a line created specifically for the burgeoning educational market. (April 29)

2003

At Macworld, Apple announces the Safari Web browser, iLife software, and new PowerBook models. Later in the month, it also announces new high-end tower units. (January 7)

Pixar releases *Finding Nemo*, which grosses $339 million domestically. It goes on to win an Academy Award for Best Animated Feature. (May 30)

Apple debuts the iTunes Music Store for Mac-only computers. (April 28)

The iTunes store opens up to Windows computer users. (October 16)

Apple debuts the Power Mac G5. (November 18)

2004

Pixar releases *The Incredibles*, which grosses $261 million domestically. It goes on to win an Academy Award for Best Animated Feature. (November 11)

SJ announces to his employees that he has pancreatic cancer and will have to undergo an operation to remove a tumor. Taking a medical leave of absence, SJ turns the reins over to Apple's head of worldwide sales and operations, Timothy D. Cook.

Early in the year, SJ's acrimonious dealings with Disney's then-CEO, Michael Eisner, created what looked to be an impassable rift regarding Pixar. SJ courts other studios, which show great interest in a partnership.

Disney CEO Michael Eisner is ousted by the board, a move orchestrated by board member Roy Disney's "Save Disney" campaign. Eisner is replaced by Disney's chief operating officer, Robert Iger, who sees Pixar as the future of Disney animation. (September)

2005

Apple introduces the Mac Mini computer at Macworld Expo in San Francisco. Later that month, Apple debuts portable PowerBook G4 computers. (January 10)

Apple develops an Intel version of Mac OS X as it prepares a permanent switch from the PowerPC platform to an Intel platform. Using Apple's new "Boot Camp" software, Windows programs will soon run on the Mac.

2006

Apple debuts the MacBook, as well as a tower unit, the Mac Pro. (January)

Disney buys Pixar for $7.4 billion; SJ gets a 7% stake in Disney, becoming its largest individual shareholder. He also becomes a member of its board of directors. (January 24)

Pixar releases *Cars*, which grosses $244 million domestically. (June 9)

SJ's gaunt-looking appearance at the annual Apple Worldwide Developers Conference (WWDC) gives rise to speculation regarding his health and Apple's succession plans.

2007

SJ announces at the Macworld Expo that he is repositioning Apple Computer Inc., as, simply, Apple, Inc. (January 9)

Apple debuts the iPhone to overwhelming public interest.

Apple debuts the Apple TV. (February)

Pixar releases *Ratatouille*, which grosses $206 million domestically. It goes on to win an Academy Award for Best Animated Feature. (June 29)

SJ is inducted into the California Hall of Fame by Governor Arnold Schwarzenegger. (December 5)

2008

Apple debuts the MacBook Air, a lightweight laptop. (January 15)

Pixar releases *WALL-E*, which grosses $223 domestically. It goes on to win an Academy Award for Best Animated Feature. (June 27)

SJ's appearance at the WWDC prompts renewed concerns about his health.

Later that month, Bloomberg prematurely releases SJ's obituary. At an Apple event SJ quotes Mark Twain, "Reports of my death are greatly exaggerated." (August 7)

2009

SJ announces to his employees, in an interoffice memo, that he is taking a six-month leave of absence due to health issues. In his absence, Timothy Cook once again takes over as acting CEO. (January 14)

At Methodist University Hospital Transplant Institute in Memphis, SJ undergoes a successful liver transplant. (April)

Pixar releases *Up*, which grosses $293 million domestically. It goes on to win an Academy Award for Best Animated Feature. (May 29)

Fortune magazine names SJ the "CEO of the decade."

2010

Pixar releases *Toy Story 3*, which grosses $415 million domestically. It goes on to win an Academy Award for Best Animated Feature. (June 18)

Apple debuts the iPad, ushering in the tablet era.

SJ creates an organ donors registry. (October)

Financial Times names SJ as its "Person of the Year."

2011

Apple opens the Mac App store. (January 6)

SJ takes an extended, open-ended leave of absence and, again, Timothy Cook takes the helm. SJ remains involved in strategic decisions. (January 17)

After years of contentious talks with the local town council in Woodside, California, SJ finally gets approval to demolish his mansion to construct an $8.45 million, 4,910-square foot home, about which architect Christopher Travis remarked to *Wired* magazine, "The site plan definitely shows unnatural restraint for a person of wealth. This kind of thing only happens when the client gives the architect specific instructions to be sparse and utilitarian." (February)

Apple debuts iPad 2. (March 2)

Mac OS 10.7, Lion, is released, bringing the look and feel of the iPhone and iPad iOS to Apple's computer line. It is available only by download as an Apple application. (July 20)

Based on Apple's market capitalization of $343 billion ($371.66 per share), it temporarily exceeds Exxon's market cap as the world's most valuable company. (August)

Apple submits a new proposal to the Cupertino City Council to build a new campus designed by Foster + Partners. Dubbed "the Spaceship" because of its round design, it will be built on 98 acres of land and be completed in 2015.

Pixar releases *Cars 2*, which grosses $189 million domestically. (as of September 2011)

Steve Jobs resigns as CEO from Apple. Timothy Cook is appointed CEO as SJ assumes the position of chairman. (August 24, 2011)

Steve Jobs, the only authorized biography of SJ, written by Walter Isaacson, moves up its publication date from March 6, 2012 to November 21, 2011. (August)

END OF AN ERA

Steve Jobs's resignation letter as CEO of Apple

August 24, 2011

To the Apple Board of Directors and the Apple Community:

I have always said if there ever came a day when I could no longer meet my duties and expectations as Apple's CEO, I would be the first to let you know. Unfortunately, that day has come.

I hereby resign as CEO of Apple. I would like to serve, if the Board sees fit, as Chairman of the Board, director and Apple employee.

As far as my successor goes, I strongly recommend that we execute our succession plan and name Tim Cook as CEO of Apple.

I believe Apple's brightest and most innovative days are ahead of it. And I look forward to watching and contributing to its success in a new role.

I have made some of the best friends of my life at Apple, and I thank you for all the many years of being able to work alongside you.

—*Steve*

CITATIONS

Anxiety before iPad Debut

Apple media event for iPhone 4.0 software, Cupertino, CA, April 8, 2010.

Apple's Core: Employees

Kara Swisher and Walt Mossberg, an interview with Bill Gates and Steve Jobs, D5 Conference: All Things Digital, Carlsbad, CA, May 30, 2007.

Apple's DNA

"'Our DNA Hasn't Changed,'" CNNMoney/*Fortune*, February 21, 2005. http://money.cnn.com/magazines/fortune/fortune_archive/2005/02/21/8251766/index.htm

Apple's Existence

Cathy Booth, David S. Jackson, and Valerie Marchant, "Steve's Job: Restart Apple," *Time*, August 18, 1997. http://www.time.com/time/magazine/article/0,9171,986849-3,00.html

Attention Getting

Characteristically used at the end of an Apple event.

Being the Best

Apple media event for iPhone 4.0 software, Cupertino, CA, April 8, 2010.

Beyond Recruiting

Rama Dev Jager and Rafael Ortiz, *In the Company of Giants: Candid Conversations with the Visionaries of Cyberspace* (New York: McGraw-Hill, 1997).

Branding

"We don't stand...", Jeffrey L. Cruikshank, *The Apple Way: 12 Management Lessons from the World's Most Innovative Company* (New York: McGraw-Hill, 2006).

"What are the great...", Cathy Booth, David S. Jackson, and Valerie Marchant, "Steve's Job: Restart Apple," *Time*, August 18, 1997. http://www.time.com/time/magazine/article/0,9171,986849-6,00.html

Broad-Based Education

Commencement address delivered at Stanford University, Stanford, CA, on June 12, 2005, which has been viewed 4.7 million times on YouTube. http://news.stanford.edu/news/2005/june15/jobs-061505.html

Broad Life Experiences, Importance of

Gary Wolf, "Steve Jobs: The Next Insanely Great Thing; The Wired Interview," *Wired*, February 1996. http://www.wired.com/wired/archive/4.02/jobs_pr.html

Company Focus

Betsy Morris, "Steve Jobs Speaks Out," CNNMoney/*Fortune*, February 2008. http://money.cnn.com/galleries/2008/fortune/0803/gallery.jobsqna.fortune/3.html

Competition

Gerald C. Lubenow and Michael Rogers, "A Whiz Kid's Fall: How Apple Computer Dumped Its Chairman,"

Newsweek, September 30, 1985. http://www.thedai-lybeast.com/newsweek/1985/09/30/jobs-talks-about-his-rise-and-fall.html

Computers

Jeff Goodell, "Steve Jobs: The Rolling Stone Interview," *Rolling Stone*, no. 684, June 16, 1994. http://www.rollingstone.com/culture/news/steve-jobs-in-1994-the-rolling-stone-interview-20110117

Computers for Everyman

Michael Krantz, David S. Jackson, Janice Maloney, and Cathy Booth, "Apple and Pixar: Steve's Two Jobs," *Time*, October 18, 1999. http://www.time.com/time/magazine/article/0,9171,992258-2,00.html

Computers as Tools

Memory & Imagination: New Pathways to the Library of Congress, directed by Michael R. Lawrence (Baltimore, MD: Michael Lawrence Films, 1990), videocassette.

Confusing Product Lines

Apple Worldwide Developers Conference, 1998.

Consumerism

"I end up...", "Steve Jobs: The guru behind Apple," *Independent*, October 29, 2005. http://www.independent.co.uk/news/science/steve-jobs-the-guru-behind-apple-513006.html

"We spent some time...", Gary Wolf, "Steve Jobs: The Next Insanely Great Thing; The Wired Interview," *Wired*, February 1996. http://www.wired.com/wired/archive/4.02/jobs_pr.html

Consumer Product Design

Softpedia, quoting excerpts from an interview by Steven Levy with Steve Jobs, on the fifth anniversary of the iPod, November 4, 2006. http://news.softpedia.com/news/Steve-Jobs-039-s-Interview-Regarding-the-5-Years-of-iPod-39397.shtml

Contribution

Anthony Imbimbo, *Steve Jobs: The Brilliant Mind Behind Apple* (Pleasantville, NY: Gareth Stevens Publishing, 2009).

Convergence

Brent Schlender, "How Big Can Apple Get?", CNNMoney/*Fortune*, February 21, 2005. http://money.cnn.com/magazines/fortune/fortune_archive/2005/02/21/8251769/index.htm

Creating New Tools

Peter Cohen and Jason Snell, "Steve Jobs at D: All Things Digital, Live Coverage," *Macworld*, May 30, 2007. http://www.macworld.com/article/58128/2007/05/steveatd.html

Creativity and Technology

Mark Millan, "How Steve Jobs' Pixar experience helped lead to Apple's iCloud," CNN Tech, June 10, 2011. http://www.cnn.com/2011/TECH/web/06/10/jobs.icloud/

Credo

"It's Not Done…", Andy Hertzfeld, "Credit Where Due," Folklore.org, January 1983. http://www.folklore.org/StoryView.py?project=Macintosh&story=Credit_Where_Due.txt&topic=Retreats&sortOrder=Sort%20by%20Date&detail=high&showcomments=1

"The Journey Is...", Andy Hertzfeld, "Credit Where Due," Folklore.org, January 1983. http://www.folklore.org/ StoryView.py?project=Macintosh&story=Credit_ Where_Due.txt&topic=Retreats&sortOrder=Sort%20 by%20Date&detail=high&showcomments=1

"The organization is clean...", Andy Reinhardt, "Steve Jobs on Apple's Resurgence: 'Not a One-Man Show,'" *Bloomberg Businessweek*, May 12, 1998. http:// www.businessweek.com/bwdaily/dnflash/may1998/ nf80512d.htm

Customer Complaints

Open letter "To all iPhone customers" on Apple Website, September 2007. http://www.apple.com/hotnews/ openiphoneletter/

Customer Loyalty

"Voices of the Innovators: The Seed of Apple's Innovation," *Bloomberg Businessweek*, October 12, 2004. http://www.businessweek.com/bwdaily/dnflash/ oct2004/nf20041012_4018_db083.htm

David versus Goliath

InfoWorld, March 8, 1982 (accessed online through Google Books).

Deadlines

"No way...", Andy Hertzfeld, "Real Artists Ship," Folklore. org, January 1984. http://www.folklore.org/StoryView. py?story=Real_Artists_Ship.txt

"Real artists...", Andy Hertzfeld, "Real Artists Ship," Folklore.org, January 1984. http://www.folklore.org/ StoryView.py?story=Real_Artists_Ship.txt

Death

"That's why I think…", David Sheff, "Playboy Interview: Steven Jobs," *Playboy*, February 1985.

"The reports of my death…", Apple media event for the iPod, Yerba Buena Center for the Performing Arts, San Francisco, September 9, 2008.

Decision Making

Karen Paik, *To Infinity and Beyond! The Story of Pixar Animation Studios* (San Francisco: Chronicle Books, 2007).

Demise

Cathy Booth, David S. Jackson, and Valerie Marchant, "Steve's Job: Restart Apple," *Time*, August 18, 1997. http://www.time.com/time/magazine/article/0,9171,986849-2,00.html

Dent in the Universe

"Jobs vs. Gates: A thirty year war," CNNMoney/*Fortune*, originally from an interview in the *Wall Street Journal*, May 25, 1993. http://money.cnn.com/galleries/2008/fortune/0806/gallery.gates_v_jobs.fortune/2.html

Design

"In most people's vocabularies…", "Apple's One-Dollar-a-Year Man," CNNMoney/*Fortune*, January 24, 2000. http://money.cnn.com/magazines/fortune/fortune_archive/2000/01/24/272277/

"Design is a funny word…", Gary Wolf, "Steve Jobs: The Next Insanely Great Thing; The Wired Interview," *Wired*, February 1996. http://www.wired.com/wired/archive/4.02/jobs.html

"Look at the Mercedes...", John Sculley with John A. Byrne, *Odyssey: Pepsi to Apple: A Journey of Adventure, Ideas, and the Future* (New York: HarperCollins, 1987).

Difference, the Essential

Owen W. Linzmayer, *Apple Confidential 2.0: The Definitive History of the World's Most Colorful Company* (San Francisco: No Starch Press, 2004).

Disney's Animated Movie Sequels

Associated Press, "As Pixar posts record earnings, ex-partner slammed," msnbc.com, from an Apple conference call in 2004. http://www.msnbc.msn.com/id/4176887/ns/business-personal_finance/t/jobs-blasts-disney-failed-movie-deal/#.Tkqt_HMSphs

E-Book Readers

David Pogue, "Steve Jobs on Amazon and Ice Cream," *New York Times*: Bits, September 9, 2009. http://bits.blogs.nytimes.com/2009/09/09/in-qa-steve-jobs-snipes-at-amazon-and-praises-ice-cream/

Employee Motivation

David Sheff, "Playboy Interview: Steven Jobs," *Playboy*, February 1985.

Employee Potential

Betsy Morris, "Steve Jobs Speaks Out," CNNMoney/*Fortune*, February 2008. http://money.cnn.com/galleries/2008/fortune/0803/gallery.jobsqna.fortune/5.html

Excellence

Jeffrey S. Young, *Steve Jobs: The Journey is the Reward* (New York: Lynx Books, 1988).

Excitement

Owen W. Linzmayer, *Apple Confidential 2.0: The Definitive History of the World's Most Colorful Company* (San Francisco: No Starch Press, 2004), 294.

Firing Employees

Daniel Morrow, Smithsonian Institution Oral and Video Histories, "Interview with Steve Jobs," conducted at NeXT Computer corporate HQ, April 20, 1995. http://americanhistory.si.edu/collections/comphist/sj1.html

Flash Crash

"Thoughts on Flash," statement on Apple Website, April 2010.

Focus

Apple Worldwide Developers Conference, San Jose Convention Center, CA, May 13–16, 1997.

Focusing on Product

"You need a very product-oriented...", "Voice of the Innovators: The Seed of Apple's Innovation," *Bloomberg Businessweek*, October 12, 2004. http://www.businessweek.com/bwdaily/dnflash/oct2004/nf20041012_4018_db083.htm

"Sure, what we do...", Stephen Fry, "The iPad Launch: Can Steve Jobs Do It Again?" *Time*, April 1, 2010. http://www.time.com/time/magazine/article/0,9171,1977113-4,00.html

Forcing the Issue

Lev Grossman, "How Apple Does It," *Time*, October 16, 2005. http://www.time.com/time/magazine/article/0,9171,1118384-1,00.html

Forward Thinking

"If you want...", David Sheff, "Playboy Interview: Steven Jobs," *Playboy*, February 1985.

"Let's go invent...", Kara Swisher and Walt Mossberg, an interview with Bill Gates and Steve Jobs, D5 Conference: All Things Digital, Carlsbad, CA, May 30, 2007. http://allthingsd.com/20070530/d5-gates-jobs-interview/

Getting It Right

Jerry Useem, "Apple: America's best retailer," CNNMoney/*Fortune*, March 8, 2007. http://money.cnn.com/magazines/fortune/fortune_archive/2007/03/19/8402321/

Goals

Michael Moritz, *Return to the Little Kingdom* (New York: Overlook Press, 2009).

Grace Under Pressure

Rama Dev Jager and Rafael Ortiz, *In the Company of Giants: Candid Conversations with the Visionaries of Cyberspace* (New York: McGraw-Hill, 1997).

Great Ideas

Transcript from the television program *Triumph of the Nerds*, PBS, airdate June 1996. http://www.pbs.org/nerds/part3.html

Great Product Design

Gary Wolf, "Steve Jobs: The Next Insanely Great Thing; The Wired Interview," *Wired*, February 1996. http://www.wired.com/wired/archive/4.02/jobs_pr.html

Great Products

"Actually, making an insanely...", David Sheff, "Playboy Interview: Steven Jobs," *Playboy*, February 1985.

"You know, my philosophy is...", Gerald C. Lubenow and Michael Rogers, "Jobs Talks About His Rise and Fall," *Newsweek*, September 29, 1985. http://www.thedailybeast.com/newsweek/1985/09/30/jobs-talks-about-his-rise-and-fall.html

Hard Work

Brent Schlender, "The Three Faces of Steve...", CNNMoney/*Fortune*, November 9, 1998. http://money.cnn.com/magazines/fortune/fortune_archive/1998/11/09/250880/

Health Speculation

Open letter to Apple community, "Letter from Apple CEO Steve Jobs," on Apple Website, January 5, 2009. http://www.apple.com/pr/library/2009/01/05Letter-from-Apple-CEO-Steve-Jobs.html

Health, Taking Time Off for

Apple media advisory to all Apple employees, January 14, 2009.

IBM

"Welcome, IBM." Apple print ad in the *Wall Street Journal*, August 24, 1981.

"IBM wants...", *Fortune*, February 20, 1984.

iCEO

Owen W. Linzmayer, *Apple Confidential 2.0: The Definitive History of the World's Most Colorful Company* (San Francisco: No Starch Press, 2004).

Impact, in an Address to Apple Employees

Michael Moritz, *Return to the Little Kingdom* (New York: Overlook Press, 2009).

Innovation

"A lot of companies...", John H. Ostdick, "Steve Jobs: Master of Innovation," *Success*, June 2010.

"Innovation distinguishes...", Carmine Gallo, *The Innovation Secrets of Steve Jobs: Insanely Different Principles for Breakthrough Success* (New York: McGraw-Hill, 2011).

"They were able to...", Jeff Goodell, "Steve Jobs: The Rolling Stone Interview," *Rolling Stone*, no. 684, June 16, 1994. http://www.rollingstone.com/culture/news/steve-jobs-in-1994-the-rolling-stone-interview-20110117

"The people who go...", Karen Paik, *To Infinity and Beyond! The Story of Pixar Animation Studios* (San Francisco: Chronicle Books, 2007).

Insight

"I think the artistry...", Daniel Morrow, Smithsonian Institution Oral and Video Histories, "Interview with Steve Jobs," conducted at NeXT Computer corporate HQ, April 20, 1995. http://americanhistory.si.edu/collections/comphist/sj1.html

"We had the hardware...", Steven Levy, "Good for the Soul," *Newsweek*, October 16, 2006. http://ashim.wordpress.com/category/inspiring/

Inspiration

Daniel Morrow, Smithsonian Institution Oral and Video Histories, "Interview with Steve Jobs," conducted at NeXT Computer corporate HQ, April 20, 1995. http://americanhistory.si.edu/collections/comphist/sj1.html

Integration

Michael Krantz, "Steve Jobs at 44," *Time*, October 10, 1999. http://www.time.com/time/magazine/article/0,9171,32207,00.html

Interdisciplinary Talents

Michael Krantz, "Steve Jobs at 44," *Time*, October 10, 1999. http://www.time.com/time/magazine/article/0,9171,32207-3,00.html

Internet Theft and Motivation

"We said: We don't...", Jeff Goodell, "Steve Jobs: The Rolling Stone Interview," *Rolling Stone*, no. 684, June 16, 1994. http://www.rollingstone.com/culture/news/steve-jobs-in-1994-the-rolling-stone-interview-20110117

"None of this technology...", Jeff Goodell, "Steve Jobs: The Rolling Stone Interview," *Rolling Stone*, no. 684, June 16, 1994. http://www.rollingstone.com/culture/news/steve-jobs-in-1994-the-rolling-stone-interview-20110117

iPad and Inevitable Change

Kara Swisher and Walt Mossberg, "Apple CEO Steve Jobs at D8: The Full, Uncut Interview," D8 Conference, All Things Digital, Rancho Palos Verdes, CA, June 1–3, 2010. http://allthingsd.com/20100607/steve-jobs-at-d8-the-full-uncut-interview/?refcat=d8

iPad Inspires iPhone

Kara Swisher and Walt Mossberg, "Apple CEO Steve Jobs at D8: The Full, Uncut Interview," D8 Conference, All Things Digital, Rancho Palos Verdes, CA, June 1–3, 2010. http://allthingsd.com/20100607/steve-jobs-at-d8-the-full-uncut-interview/?refcat=d8

iPhone

Steven Levy, "Apple Computer Is Dead; Long Live Apple," *Newsweek*, January 9, 2007. http://www.the-dailybeast.com/newsweek/2007/01/09/steven-levy-apple-computer-is-dead-long-live-apple.html

iPod Nano

"CNBC Steve Jobs September 2006," YouTube video, 3:40, from the Apple Keynote address at the Yerba Buena Center for the Arts Theater, San Francisco, CA, September 12, 2006, reported by Jim Goldman, CNBC Business News. http://www.youtube.com/watch?v=r7wXWDrvjoM

iPod Touch

David Pogue, "Steve Jobs on Amazon and Ice Cream," *New York Times*: Bits, September 9, 2009. http://bits.blogs.nytimes.com/2009/09/09/in-qa-steve-jobs-snipes-at-amazon-and-praises-ice-cream/

iTunes

"Apple Special Event [Sep 12, 2006] - (1/6)," YouTube video, 12:46, from the Apple Keynote address at the Yerba Buena Center for the Arts Theater, San Francisco, CA, September 12, 2006. The remaining five parts of the speech are also available on YouTube. http://www.youtube.com/watch?v=d2t_66RF37U

Jobs's *Curriculum Vitae* (Résumé)

Steve Jobs's résumé, originally posted on www.me.com.
Though it has since been removed, it can still be
found reposted on many Websites. http://100legends.
blogspot.com/2011/01/steve-jobs-resume.html

Jobs's Legacy at Apple

Gerald C. Lubenow and Michael Rogers, "Jobs Talks
About His Rise and Fall," *Newsweek*, September
29, 1985. http://www.thedailybeast.com/news-
week/1985/09/30/jobs-talks-about-his-rise-and-fall.
html

Jobs's $1 Annual Salary

Katie Marsal, "Jobs: 'I make fifty cents just for showing
up,'" *Apple Insider*, May 10, 2007. http://www.applein-
sider.com/articles/07/05/10/jobs_i_make_fifty_cents_
just_for_showing_up.html

Letting Go of the Past

Steven Levy, "25 Years of Mac: From Boxy Beige to Silver
Sleek," *Wired*, no. 17.01, December 22, 2008. http://
www.wired.com/techbiz/it/magazine/17-01/ff_mac

Life's Complications

"Steve Jobs: The guru behind Apple," *The Independent*, October 29, 2005. http://www.independent.
co.uk/news/science/steve-jobs-the-guru-behind-
apple-513006.html

Losing Market Share

"Voice of the Innovators: The Seed of Apple's Innovation," *Bloomberg Businessweek*, October 12, 2004. http://www.businessweek.com/bwdaily/dnflash/oct2004/nf20041012_4018_db083.htm

Losing Money

Owen W. Linzmayer, *Apple Confidential 2.0: The Definitive History of the World's Most Colorful Company* (San Francisco: No Starch Press, 2004).

Lost Opportunities

David Brier, "Like Life, Branding Needs Vision Too," *Fast Company*, August 11, 2009. http://www.fastcompany.com/blog/david-brier/defying-gravity-and-rising-above-noise/life-branding-needs-vision-too

Mac Cube

Macworld Expo, New York City, 2000.

Mac's Introduction

Apple Special Event for the Macintosh, January 1984.

Mac Legacy

Daniel Morrow, Smithsonian Institution Oral and Video Histories, "Interview with Steve Jobs," conducted at NeXT Computer corporate HQ, April 20, 1995. http://americanhistory.si.edu/collections/comphist/sj1.html

Making Bold Announcements

Steve Kemper, "Steve Jobs and Jeff Bezos meet 'Ginger,'" excerpt from *Code Name Ginger*, Harvard Business School *Working Knowledge for Business Leaders*, June 16, 2003. http://hbswk.hbs.edu/archive/3533.html

Marketing

John Sculley with John A. Byrne, *Odyssey: Pepsi to Apple: A Journey of Adventure, Ideas, and the Future* (New York: HarperCollins, 1987). Apple Expo Paris, media interview, September 20, 2005.

Microsoft's Lack of Innovation

"The only problem...", transcript from the television program *Triumph of the Nerds*, PBS, airdate June 1996. http://www.pbs.org/nerds/part3.html

"The thing I don't think...", Jeff Goodell, "Steve Jobs: The Rolling Stone Interview," *Rolling Stone*, no. 684, June 16, 1994. http://www.rollingstone.com/culture/news/steve-jobs-in-1994-the-rolling-stone-interview-20110117

Microsoft's Microview

Steve Lohr, "Creating Jobs: Apple's Founder Goes Home Again," *New York Times Magazine*, January 12, 1997. http://partners.nytimes.com/library/cyber/week/011897jobs.html?scp=1&sq=steve%20jobs%20apple's%20founder%20goes%20home%20again&st=cse

Misplaced Values

David Sheff, "Playboy Interview: Steven Jobs," *Playboy*, February 1985.

Mistakes

D8 Conference, All Things Digital, Rancho Palos Verdes, CA, June 1–3, 2010.

Money

"Innovation has nothing to do…", David Kirkpatrick
and Tyler Maroney, "The Second Coming of Apple
Through a magical fusion of man—Steve Jobs—and
company, Apple is becoming itself again: the little
anticompany that could," CNNMoney/*Fortune*, November 9, 1998. http://money.cnn.com/magazines/for-
tune/fortune_archive/1998/11/09/250834/index.htm

"I was worth…", transcript from the television program
Triumph of the Nerds, PBS, airdate June 1996. http://
www.pbs.org/nerds/part1.html

Motivating Employees

"What happens in most companies…", David Sheff, "Playboy Interview: Steven Jobs," *Playboy*, February 1985.

"The people who are doing…", *Macworld*, no. 1, February 1984. http://www.macworld.com/arti-
cle/29181/2004/02/themacturns20jobs.html

Motivation

"Do you want to spend…", John Sculley with John A.
Byrne, *Odyssey: Pepsi to Apple: A Journey of Adventure, Ideas, and the Future* (New York: HarperCollins,
1987).

"It's better to be a pirate…", John Sculley with John A.
Byrne, *Odyssey: Pepsi to Apple: A Journey of Adventure, Ideas, and the Future* (New York: HarperCollins,
1987).

"You could spend billions…", Cathy Booth, David S.
Jackson, and Valerie Marchant, "Steve's Job: Restart
Apple," *Time*, August 19, 1997. http://www.time.com/
time/magazine/article/0,9171,986849-6,00.html

Need for Teamwork

Daniel Morrow, Smithsonian Institution Oral and Video Histories, "Interview with Steve Jobs," conducted at NeXT Computer corporate HQ, April 20, 1995. http://americanhistory.si.edu/collections/comphist/sj1.html

Netbooks

Apple's launch event for iPad 1, Yerba Buena Center For the Arts, San Francisco, CA, January 27, 2010.

New Products

Apple's launch event for iPad 2, Yerba Buena Center For the Arts, San Francisco, CA, March 2, 2011.

No Resting on Laurels

Brian Williams, "Steve Jobs: Iconoclast and salesman: Apple founder's newest store wows fans in Manhattan," msnbc.com, May 25, 2006. http://www.msnbc.msn.com/id/12974884/ns/nightly_news/t/steve-jobs-iconoclast-salesman/#.TkwtIXMSphs

Owning the User Experience

Josh Quittner and Rebecca Winters, "Apple's New Core," *Time*, January 14, 2002. http://www.time.com/time/magazine/article/0,9171,1001600-6,00.html

Packaging

Paul Kunkel and Rick English, *AppleDesign: The Work of the Apple Industrial Design Group* (New York: Graphis, 1997).

PARC's Graphical Interface

Daniel Morrow, Smithsonian Institution Oral and Video Histories, "Interview with Steve Jobs," conducted at NeXT Computer corporate HQ, April 20, 1995. http://americanhistory.si.edu/collections/comphist/sj1.html

PARC's Innovations

Daniel Morrow, Smithsonian Institution Oral and Video Histories, "Interview with Steve Jobs," conducted at NeXT Computer corporate HQ, April 20, 1995. http://americanhistory.si.edu/collections/comphist/sj1.html

Parochial Thinking

Bobbie Johnson, "The coolest player in town," *Guardian*, September 22, 2005. http://www.guardian.co.uk/technology/2005/sep/22/stevejobs.guardianweeklytechnologysection

Partnership

Kara Swisher and Walt Mossberg, an interview with Bill Gates and Steve Jobs, D5 Conference: All Things Digital, Carlsbad, CA, May 30, 2007. http://allthingsd.com/20071224/best-of-2007-video-d5-interview-with-bill-gates-and-steve-jobs/?refcat=d5

Passion

"People say you have to...", Kara Swisher and Walt Mossberg, an interview with Bill Gates and Steve Jobs, D5 Conference: All Things Digital, Carlsbad, CA, May 30, 2007. http://allthingsd.com/20071224/best-of-2007-video-d5-interview-with-bill-gates-and-steve-jobs/?refcat=d5

"You've got to find...", commencement address delivered at Stanford University, Stanford, CA, June 12, 2005. http://news.stanford.edu/news/2005/june15/jobs-061505.html

Passive versus Active Thinking

Jason Snell, "Steve Jobs on the Mac's 20th Anniversary," *Macworld*, February 2, 2004. http://www.macworld.com/article/29181/2004/02/themacturns20jobs.html

PC as the Digital Hub

Josh Quittner and Rebecca Winters, "Apple's New Core," *Time*, January 14, 2002. http://www.time.com/time/magazine/article/0,9171,192601,00.html

Perception

Jeff Goodell, "Steve Jobs: The Rolling Stone Interview," *Rolling Stone*, no. 684, June 16, 1994. http://www.rollingstone.com/culture/news/steve-jobs-in-1994-the-rolling-stone-interview-20110117

Perseverance

Daniel Morrow, Smithsonian Institution Oral and Video Histories, "Interview with Steve Jobs," conducted at NeXT Computer corporate HQ, April 20, 1995. http://americanhistory.si.edu/collections/comphist/sj1.html

Pixar

"Pixar's got by far...", Daniel Morrow, Smithsonian Institution Oral and Video Histories, "Interview with Steve Jobs," conducted at NeXT Computer corporate HQ, April 20, 1995. http://americanhistory.si.edu/collections/comphist/sj1.html

"We believe....", Brent Schlender and Jane Furth, "Steve Jobs' amazing movie adventure: Disney is betting on computerdom's ex-boy wonder to deliver this year's animated Christmas blockbuster. Can he do for Hollywood what he did for Silicon Valley?", CNNMoney/*Fortune*, September 18, 1995. http://money.cnn.com/magazines/fortune/fortune_archive/1995/09/18/206099/index.htm

Pixar's People

Brent Schlender, "The Three Faces of Steve. In this exclusive, personal conversation, Apple's CEO reflects on the turnaround, and how a wunderkind become an old pro," CNNMoney/*Fortune*, November 9, 1998. http://money.cnn.com/magazines/fortune/fortune_archive/1998/11/09/250880/

Porn Apps on Android

Apple media event for iPhone 4.0 software, April 8, 2010, Cupertino, CA.

Pride in Product

Andy Hertzfeld, "Signing Party," Folklore.org, February 1982. Of the 47 signatures, one stands out because it's signed all in lower case—Steve Jobs's. http://www.folklore.org/StoryView.py?project=Macintosh&story=Signing_Party.txt&topic=Apple%20Spirit&sortOrder=Sort%20by%20Date

Priorities Assessment

Steve Lohr, "Creating Jobs: Apple's Founder Goes
    Home Again," *New York Times Magazine*, Janu-
    ary 12, 1997. http://partners.nytimes.com/library/
    cyber/week/011897jobs.html?scp=1&sq=steve%20
    jobs%20apple's%20founder%20goes%20home%20
    again&st=cse

Process

"Voices of the Innovators: The Seed of Apple's Innova-
    tion," *Bloomberg Businessweek*, October 12, 2004.
    http://www.businessweek.com/bwdaily/dnflash/
    oct2004/nf20041012_4018_PG2_db083.htm

Products

"Steve Jobs' Magic Kingdom: How Apple's demanding
    visionary will shake up Disney and the world of en-
    tertainment," *Bloomberg Businessweek*, February 6,
    2006. http://www.businessweek.com/magazine/con-
    tent/06_06/b3970001.htm

Product Creation

Jim Goldman, "Interview Transcript: Steve Jobs," CNBC.
    com, September 5, 2007. http://www.cnbc.com/
    id/20610975/Interview_Transcript_Steve_Jobs

Product Design

Brent Schlender and Christine Y. Chen, "Steve Jobs'
    Apple Gets Way Cooler...," CNNMoney/*Fortune*,
    January 24, 2000. http://money.cnn.com/magazines/
    fortune/fortune_archive/2000/01/24/272281/index.
    htm

Product Imagination

Betsy Morris, "Steve Jobs Speaks Out," CNNMoney/
Fortune, February 2008. http://money.cnn.com/galleries/2008/fortune/0803/gallery.jobsqna.fortune/2.html

Product Innovation

"The Steve Jobs Way: A relentless pursuit of perfection," CNN.com, April 23, 2004. http://edition.cnn.com/2004/WORLD/americas/04/16/jobs/

Product Integration

"The things I'm most proud...", Daniel Morrow, Smithsonian Institution Oral and Video Histories, "Interview with Steve Jobs," conducted at NeXT Computer corporate HQ, April 20, 1995. http://americanhistory.si.edu/collections/comphist/sj1.html

"Apple has a core set of talents...", Jeff Goodell, "Steve Jobs: The Rolling Stone Interview," *Rolling Stone*, no. 684, June 16, 1994. http://www.rollingstone.com/culture/news/steve-jobs-in-1994-the-rolling-stone-interview-20110117

"Apple is the most creative...", Peter Burrows, Ronald Grover, and Tom Lowry, "Show Time!," *Bloomberg Businessweek*, February 2, 2004. http://www.businessweek.com/magazine/content/04_05/b3868001_mz001.htm

"One company makes...", Lev Grossman, "How Apple Does it," *Time*, October 16, 2005. http://www.time.com/time/magazine/article/0,9171,1118384-3,00.html

Product Secrecy

Jake Tapper, "Interview with Apple CEO Steve Jobs," ABCNews.com podcast transcript, June 29, 2005. http://abcnews.go.com/Technology/story?id=892335&page=2

Products' Appeal

David Sheff, "Playboy Interview: Steven Jobs," *Playboy*, February 1985.

Profit Sharing, Not Advances

Jeff Goodell, "Steve Jobs: The Rolling Stone Interview," *Rolling Stone,* December 3, 2003. http://www.keystonemac.com/pdfs/Steve_Jobs_Interview.pdf

Quality

"We just wanted…", David Sheff, "Playboy Interview: Steven Jobs," *Playboy*, February 1985.

"Quality is more…", Peter Burrows, Ronald Grover, and Heather Green, "Steve Jobs' Magic Kingdom: How Apple's demanding visionary will shake up Disney and the world of entertainment," *Bloomberg Businessweek*, February 6, 2006. http://www.businessweek.com/magazine/content/06_06/b3970001.htm

Real Estate Location

Jerry Useem, "Apple: America's best retailer," CNNMoney/*Fortune*, March 8, 2007. http://money.cnn.com/magazines/fortune/fortune_archive/2007/03/19/8402321/

Reliability

Characteristically used at Apple product events.

Repeating Success

Karen Paik, *To Infinity and Beyond! The Story of Pixar Animation Studios* (San Francisco: Chronicle Books, 2007).

Risking Failure

Brent Schlender, "The Three Faces of Steve. In this exclusive, personal conversation, Apple's CEO reflects on the turnaround, and on how a wunderkind became an old pro," CNNMoney/*Fortune*, November 9, 1998. http://money.cnn.com/magazines/fortune/fortune_archive/1998/11/09/250880/

Shared Vision

Daniel Morrow, Smithsonian Institution Oral and Video Histories, "Interview with Steve Jobs," conducted at NeXT Computer corporate HQ, April 20, 1995. http://americanhistory.si.edu/collections/comphist/sj1.html

Simplicity

"As technology becomes…", Rob Walker, "The Guts of a New Machine," *New York Times Magazine*, November 30, 2003. http://www.nytimes.com/2003/11/30/magazine/30IPOD.html?pagewanted=all

"If we could make…", keynote address, Seybold Seminars, New York, March 1998.

"There's a very strong DNA…", Bobbie Johnson, "The coolest player in town," *Guardian*, September 22, 2005. http://www.guardian.co.uk/technology/2005/sep/22/stevejobs.guardianweeklytechnologysection

"If you go out and ask…", Sonny Lim, "The Steve Jobs Interview," Macworld Expo, Tokyo, March 13, 1999. http://www.advergence.com/news-page/1999/19990314_stevejobs.cna.shtml

"We've reviewed...", keynote address, Macworld Expo, January 6, 1998.

"Mobile devices are really...", Jefferson Graham, "Q&A: Apple's Steve Jobs and AT&T's Randall Stephenson," *USA Today: Technology*, July 28, 2007.

Slogan: First Generation iPod

Apple advertisement, October 31, 2001.

Software

"Bill [Gates]...", Kara Swisher and Walt Mossberg, an interview with Bill Gates and Steve Jobs, D5 Conference: All Things Digital, Carlsbad, CA, May 30, 2007. http://allthingsd.com/20070531/d5-gates-jobs-transcript/

"What's really interesting...", Kara Swisher and Walt Mossberg, an interview with Bill Gates and Steve Jobs, D5 Conference: All Things Digital, Carlsbad, CA, May 30, 2007. http://allthingsd.com/20070531/d5-gates-jobs-transcript/

"It makes your camcorder...", keynote speech at Macworld, Moscone Convention Center, San Francisco, CA, January 9, 2001.

Soul of the New Machine

Apple Worldwide Developers Conference, Moscone Convention Center, San Francisco, CA, June 6–10, 2011. http://www.youtube.com/watch?v=3lsMFzxtSZ8

Stagnation, the Danger of

Owen W. Linzmayer, *Apple Confidential 2.0: The Definitive History of the World's Most Colorful Company* (San Francisco: No Starch Press, 2004).

Stickiness

Leander Kahney, *Inside Steve's Brain* (New York: Penguin Group, 2009).

Stock Options

Brent Schlender, "The Three Faces of Steve," CNNMoney/*Fortune*, November 9, 1998. http://money.cnn.com/magazines/fortune/fortune_archive/1998/11/09/250880/

Story, Importance of

Karen Paik, *To Infinity and Beyond! The Story of Pixar Animation Studios* (San Francisco: Chronicle Books, 2007).

Strategy

Brent Schlender and Jane Furth, "Steve Jobs' Amazing Movie Adventure...", CNNMoney/*Fortune*, September 18, 1995.

Success

Karen Paik, *To Infinity and Beyond! The Story of Pixar Animation Studios* (San Francisco: Chronicle Books, 2007).

Sucker-Punched, Being

David Sheff, "Playboy Interview: Steven Jobs," *Playboy*, February 1985.

Survival

Josh Quittner, "Apple's New Core," *Time*, February 5, 2003. http://www.time.com/time/business/article/0,8599,190914,00.html

Takeovers, Hostile

Josh Quittner, "Apple's New Core," *Time*, February 5, 2003. http://www.time.com/time/business/article/0,8599,190914,00.html

Taking Stock of Apple

Cathy Booth, David S. Jackson, and Valerie Marchant, "Steve's Job: Restart Apple," *Time*, August 18, 1997. http://www.time.com/time/magazine/article/0,9171,986849-3,00.html

Teamwork

"Steve Jobs," video clip, 1:11, from a video interview with *60 Minutes*, March 4, 2009. http://www.cbsnews.com/video/watch/?id=4835857n

Technology in Perspective

Charles Arthur, "Steve Jobs: The Guru Behind Apple," *The Independent:* Science, October 29, 2005. http://www.independent.co.uk/news/science/steve-jobs-the-guru-behind-apple-513006.html

"Think Different" Ad Campaign

Sonny Lim, "Transcript: The Steve Jobs Interview," an interview from Channel NewsAsia conducted at Macworld Expo, Tokyo, March 13, 1999. http://www.advergence.com/newspage/1999/19990314_stevejobs.cna.shtml

Thinking Through the Problem

"Once you get into the problem…", Paul Kunkel and Rick English, *AppleDesign: The Work of the Apple Industrial Design Group* (New York: Graphis, 1997).

"We have a lot of customers...", Andy Reinhardt, "Steve Jobs: 'There's Sanity Returning,'" *Bloomberg Businessweek*, May 25, 1998. http://www.businessweek.com/1998/21/b3579165.htm

To Be or Not to Be

Commencement address delivered at Stanford University, Stanford, CA, on June 12, 2005. http://news.stanford.edu/news/2005/june15/jobs-061505.html

Toy Story 2

Karen Paik, *To Infinity and Beyond! The Story of Pixar Animation Studios* (San Francisco: Chronicle Books, 2007).

Trash Talking

Owen W. Linzmayer, *Apple Confidential 2.0: The Definitive History of the World's Most Colorful Company* (San Francisco: No Starch Press, 2004).

Ubiquity of Mac

Jeff Goodell, "Steve Jobs: The Rolling Stone Interview," *Rolling Stone*, December 3, 2003. http://www.keystonemac.com/pdfs/Steve_Jobs_Interview.pdf

User Experience

"'Our DNA Hasn't Changed,'" CNNMoney/*Fortune*, February 21, 2005. http://money.cnn.com/magazines/fortune/fortune_archive/2005/02/21/8251766/index.htm

Values

Michael Moritz, *Return to the Little Kingdom* (New York: Overlook Press, 2009).

Vision

"We're gambling on...", Apple product event for the first Macintosh computer, January 24, 1984.

"I'm always keeping...", Brent Schlender and Christine Y. Chen, "Steve Jobs' Apple Gets Way Cooler...," CNNMoney/*Fortune*, January 24, 2000. http://money.cnn.com/magazines/fortune/fortune_archive/2000/01/24/272281/index.htm

Wisdom

"The Classroom of the Future," *Newsweek*, October 28, 2001. http://www.thedailybeast.com/newsweek/2001/10/28/the-classroom-of-the-future.html

Working Hard and Growing Older

Michael Krantz, "Steve Jobs at 44," *Time*, October 10, 1999. http://www.time.com/time/magazine/article/0,9171,32207-4,00.html

Zen

Commencement address delivered at Stanford University, Stanford, CA, June 12, 2005. Shunryu Suzuki's popular saying is from *Zen Mind, Beginner's Mind* (Boston: Shambhala Publications, 2006). http://news.stanford.edu/news/2005/june15/jobs-061505.html

ABOUT THE EDITOR

George Beahm has published more than thirty books on a variety of subjects, including business and popular culture. He lives in southeast Virginia.

Beahm is a former U.S. Army Field Artillery officer who served on active duty in the National Guard and in the Army Reserves.

His website is www.georgebeahm.com.